A Three Days' Journey

The Distance Between Egypt and Glory

Chris Carter

Going Pastoral

PREFACE

This book began in the pulpit, but it was shaped in the wilderness.

For more than three decades I have served as a pastor in Mississippi, and for most of those years I have carried a quiet, growing burden that I could not fully put into words until now. Sunday after Sunday I watched sincere believers sing with conviction, pray with feeling, and then walk back into a Monday world that looked indistinguishable from the lives of people who had never opened a Bible. The gap between worship and daily life was not a gap of sincerity. These were not hypocrites. They were faithful people who loved God and genuinely wanted to follow Him. Yet something was off, and both they and I could feel it. The faith we professed and the lives we lived were not as close as they should have been, and the distance between them seemed to be widening rather than narrowing.

I wrestled with that distance in my own life first. As a bivocational pastor who also serves in the logistics division of a Christian, family-owned building-products manufacturer, I know what it is to move between the sanctuary and the workplace, between sermon preparation and spreadsheets, between counseling sessions and compliance audits. I know how easily the values of the surrounding culture press themselves into a life that is already full, already tired, already running on fumes. Materialism does not announce itself with trumpets. It arrives disguised as responsibility. Entertainment does not feel like spiritual numbing. It feels like rest you have earned. The idols of our age are effective precisely because they do not look like idols, and I have had to confront them in my own heart before I could ever write honestly about them for someone else.

The turning point came as I studied the Exodus narratives more carefully than I ever had. When Moses stood before Pharaoh, the request God gave him was remarkably specific: "Let us go a three days' journey into the wilderness, that we may sacrifice to the Lord our God." Not a vague plea for freedom. A precise demand for distance. God insisted that His people could not truly worship Him while remaining inside Egypt's system, surrounded by Egypt's gods, shaped by Egypt's values. Worship required departure. Encounter required separation. And that separation was not a retreat into irrelevance but a journey toward the only place where genuine transformation could happen.

That pattern broke open the Scriptures for me in a way I had not experienced before. I began to see the same call echoing from Abraham's departure from Ur to the prophets' warnings about Babylon, from Jesus' prayer that His followers be kept from the world's grip to the voice in Revelation crying, "Come out of her, My people." The Bible is, from beginning to end, the story of a God who calls His people out of corrupting systems so that He can bring them into something better. And the Greek word the New Testament uses for the church—ekklesia, "called-out ones"—carries that truth in its very letters. Separation is not an optional feature of Christian maturity. It is woven into the identity of what it means to belong to God's people at all.

As these convictions deepened, so did a pastoral urgency. I looked around and saw believers embedded in materialism they had not named, numbed by entertainment they had not questioned, shaped by political allegiances and inherited traditions they had never held up to the light of Scripture. I saw worship cultures built more on spectacle and emotional stimulation than on the presence and Word of God. I saw end-times anxiety producing fear and division rather than holiness and hope. And I saw myself reflected in every one of those patterns. This book is not written from a position above the struggle. It is written from inside it.

My first book, Grace in Everyday Relationships: A Practical Guide for Navigating Everyday Relationships with Grace, grew out of years of walking with people through the relational trenches of marriage, family, friendship, and the workplace. That book addressed how the grace of Christ reshapes the way we speak, forgive, set boundaries, and persevere with one another. This book addresses something that lies beneath and behind all of those relationships: the question of who and what we are actually living for. If Grace in Everyday Relationships was about how we relate to the people closest to us, A Three Days' Journey is about the deeper allegiance that makes those relationships either fruitful or hollow. It asks whether we have truly left Egypt, or whether we are still trying to worship God while surrounded by idols we have grown too comfortable to see.

Writing this book has also been, for me, one concrete way to love God and love my neighbor. Jesus tells us that all the Law and the Prophets hang on those two great commandments. I cannot preach in every pulpit, sit in every counseling room, or enter every living room where the Sunday-to-Monday gap hangs in the air. But I can offer what I have—years of pastoral observation, personal failure, biblical study, and hard-won course corrections—in a form that can travel farther than I ever could on my own. This book is one of the ways I have chosen to participate in that double calling: to love the Lord with all my heart, soul, mind, and strength, and to love my neighbor as myself by contributing something that might help them name what needs to be named, leave what needs to be left, and walk into the wilderness where God does His deepest work.

My hope is that this book will, in some small but real way, make a positive difference. I do not imagine that a single volume can uproot every idol that has taken years to grow. But I do believe that God delights to use simple, biblical truth—applied patiently and specifically—to awaken hearts, clarify allegiances, and make room for the kind of life that actually looks different from the surrounding culture. If even a handful of believers begin to see the Egypt they have been living in, if a few churches recover a vision of worship that transforms rather than merely entertains, if one reader finds the courage to step into the wilderness and discovers that God meets them there with a faithfulness that Egypt could never offer, then the labor of writing will have been well spent.

If you are picking up this book because something in your spiritual life feels hollow, familiar, or uncomfortably ordinary, you are not alone—and you are not without hope. The same God who called Abraham out of Ur, who led Israel through the Red Sea, and who raised Jesus from the grave on the third day is calling still. His voice has not changed. His offer has not expired. And the distance between where you are and where He wants to take you is not a punishment. It is an invitation.

Come out. There is something better waiting on the other side of your departure.

Contents

INTRODUCTION

Introduction

Something is wrong, and most believers can feel it even if they can't name it.

They go to church on Sunday. They sing the songs. They raise their hands. They say amen. Then Monday comes, and the same anxieties that drive their non-Christian neighbors drive them too. The same materialism. The same hunger for entertainment. The same quiet dread about money, status, and whether life is turning out the way it was supposed to. Sunday and Monday feel like two completely different lives, and the distance between them is growing.

This book exists because that gap isn't accidental. It's the predictable result of trying to worship God without ever actually leaving Egypt.

That's not a metaphor used loosely. It's the precise diagnosis Scripture offers for the condition so many believers find themselves in right now. And understanding it changes everything.

The Call to Depart: Leaving Egypt Behind

When Moses stood before Pharaoh, the request God gave him was specific. Not "let my people go" in some vague, general sense. The exact words were: "Let us go a three days' journey into the wilderness, that we may sacrifice to the Lord our God." Three days. Into the wilderness. Away from Egypt. That was the condition God set for worship. Distance first, then encounter.

That detail is not incidental. God didn't tell Moses to ask Pharaoh if Israel could worship in Egypt, in the middle of their daily routines, surrounded by the same brick kilns and slave drivers and Egyptian gods carved into every wall. He called them out. Out of the system. Out of the environment. Out of the familiar. And only then, on the other side of that distance, would genuine worship be possible.

This pattern didn't start with Moses, and it didn't end with him either.

It started with a man named Abraham, living in a city called Ur of the Chaldees. God came to him with a command that must have felt completely unreasonable: "Get out of your country, from your family and from your father's house, to a land that I will show you" (Genesis 12:1). No map. No destination named. Just a call to leave everything familiar and walk into the unknown with nothing but God's word as a guide. Abraham went. And that act of departure became the founding moment of a people who would carry God's presence through history.

Ur of the Chaldees is worth pausing on for a moment. That city sat in the region that Scripture would later call Babylon. The very place God called Abraham out of at the beginning of redemptive history is the same spiritual system God calls His people out of at the end of it. In Revelation 18:4, the voice from heaven says, "Come out of her, my people, lest you share in her sins." From Genesis to Revelation, the call is the same. God separates His people from a corrupting system before He brings them into something better. That's not a coincidence. That's a pattern God keeps repeating because He knows something we keep forgetting: you can't fully receive what He's offering while you're still holding onto what He's asking you to release.

The word the New Testament uses for the church carries this same truth in its very letters. The Greek word is ekklesia. It literally means "called-out ones." Not "gathered ones" in a neutral sense, but those who have been specifically called out from one place and assembled somewhere else. Every time someone calls the church "the church," they're using a word that has separation built into its definition. Being part of God's people isn't just about what you've been called into. It's equally about what you've been called out of.

That's a significant thing to sit with. Separation isn't an optional feature of Christian life, something the more serious believers pursue while others settle for something softer. It's woven into the very identity of what it means to belong to God's people at all. You were called out. The question this book asks is whether you've actually gone.

Now, before that word "separation" creates the wrong picture, it needs to be clarified directly. Separation is not the same thing as isolation. The three-day journey into the wilderness wasn't a permanent retreat into irrelevance. It was a journey toward authentic encounter with God that would ultimately send Israel back into the world with something real to offer. Jesus prayed in John 17:15, "I do not pray that You should take them out of the world, but that You should keep them from the evil one." He didn't ask the Father to remove His followers from contact with culture. He asked for their protection within it. The goal of separation is never to make believers useless to the world. The goal is to make them genuinely different from it, which is the only thing that makes them genuinely useful to it.

Think about what happens to salt that dissolves completely into water. It's no longer salt. It can't flavor anything. It can't preserve anything. It's just water with a slightly different chemical composition. A Christian who has absorbed the world's values so thoroughly that nothing about their life looks or feels different from their neighbors isn't just personally weakened. They've lost the very quality that makes them able to serve the people around them.

Consider someone like Marcus, a hypothetical 38-year-old pastor's son who grew up in the church, knows his Bible well, and genuinely loves God. But over the years, without noticing it happening, his financial decisions started being driven by the same anxiety about status and security that drives everyone else in his neighborhood. His prayer life shrank as his screen time grew. His worship experience became dependent on the right lighting and the right song rather than the actual presence of God. He isn't a bad person. He isn't a hypocrite in the dramatic sense. He's just someone who tried to keep worshipping in Egypt, and slowly, Egypt started worshipping back through him. This is not a story about moral failure. It's a story about spiritual drift, and it's far more common than most Christians want to admit.

Romans 12:1-2 frames everything this book is about. "Do not conform to this world, but be transformed by the renewing of your mind." The word "conform" in the original language carries the image of being pressed into a mold. The world is always pressing. It presses through advertising that tells you what success looks like. It presses through entertainment that slowly reshapes what your soul finds satisfying. It presses through political movements that promise to restore what only God can restore. It presses through church environments built more on spectacle than on Scripture. The pressure is constant, and it's subtle enough that most people don't feel it happening. They just wake up one day and realize they look exactly like the mold.

Paul's answer to that pressure isn't to hide from it. It's transformation. A renewing of the mind so thorough that the mold no longer fits. That's what the three-day journey produces. That's what the wilderness is for. Not punishment. Not exile. Transformation.

What You Will Learn and Why It Matters

This book is going to ask you to do something specific. Not just think differently, but actually identify the places in your life where Egypt still has a claim on you. That requires honesty, and it requires the kind of courage that comes from believing the destination is worth the cost of the departure.

The first thing you'll learn to do is name the idols. Not the obvious ones carved from wood and stone, but the modern equivalents that are far more effective precisely because they don't look like idols at all. Materialism doesn't announce itself as a competing god. It announces itself as wisdom, as responsibility, as providing for your family. Entertainment doesn't feel like spiritual numbing. It feels like rest, like reward, like something you've earned after a hard week. These are the "Egyptian" structures that have become so normal they're invisible, and invisible idols are the most dangerous kind because you can't dismantle what you can't see.

You'll learn to look at your calendar and your bank account and your screen-time report not as neutral data but as a map of your actual allegiances. Where your time goes tells you what you actually worship, regardless of what you say on Sunday. Where your money flows reveals what you actually trust to give you security, significance, and satisfaction. These aren't condemnations. They're diagnostics. And a good diagnosis is always the first step toward genuine health.

You'll also learn why the Sunday-to-Monday gap exists and what closes it. The gap isn't primarily a motivation problem. It's not that believers need to try harder or feel more guilty about their inconsistency. The gap exists because the connection between worship and daily life has been severed. Worship has been reduced to an event that happens in a building on one morning per week, and life has been left to run on whatever values the surrounding culture supplies. Romans 12 calls for something entirely different: a life that is itself a sacrifice, an offering, a continuous act of worship. When that vision takes hold, Monday doesn't feel separate from Sunday anymore. They're part of the same offering.

The principles in this book aren't theoretical. They're specific. You'll come away from each chapter with a clear understanding of what needs to change and a practical path for changing it. Not vague encouragements to "seek God more" or "be in the Word," but actual, concrete steps for identifying where cultural pressure has shaped your thinking, how to create the spiritual distance needed to hear God clearly again, and what it looks like to reorient your daily life around allegiance to Christ rather than accommodation to culture.

This matters most urgently for believers who feel the gap but haven't been able to close it. The ones who are sincere. The ones who aren't walking away from faith but feel like their faith isn't walking anywhere either. If that's you, this book was written with your specific situation in mind.

The world has no shortage of voices telling Christians what they should be against. Political movements, culture warriors, online commentators all compete to tell the church who its enemies are and what battles it should be fighting. This book isn't one more voice in that crowd. The call here isn't to conquer culture or condemn it. The call is far older, far quieter, and far more demanding than that. It's the same call God gave Abraham. The same call Moses carried to Pharaoh. The same call that echoes through Revelation. Come out. Not to fight. Not to hide. But to worship in a way that's actually free.

True holiness has never been about isolation from the world or political dominance over it. It's about reoriented allegiance. It's about a life where Christ, not comfort, sits at the center. Where the question driving every decision isn't "what does this do for me?" but "what does this offer to God?" That kind of life looks different from the surrounding culture in ways that are visible, specific, and sometimes costly. And that visible difference is exactly what makes it a witness.

The Journey Ahead: From Bondage to Resurrection

The Israelites who left Egypt on the night of the Passover were in a strange position. They were no longer slaves. But they weren't yet inhabitants of the Promised Land either. They were in between. The old identity had been stripped away, but the new one hadn't fully formed yet. They were standing in what theologians sometimes call liminal space: the threshold between what was and what will be.

That in-between place is uncomfortable. It was for Israel, and it will be for you. The wilderness strips things away. It removes the props and the distractions and the familiar comforts that Egypt provided. The Israelites actually complained about this. They remembered the food in Egypt. They missed the predictability of slavery because at least in slavery they knew what each day would hold. The wilderness offered no such certainty. Just God. Just manna. Just the cloud by day and the fire by night.

And that's precisely where God did His most intimate and transformative work in them.

The wilderness chapters of this book will ask you to sit with that same discomfort. When entertainment is reduced and silence increases, the first thing that fills the silence is usually anxiety. When materialism is named as an idol and you begin to loosen its grip, the first feeling is often insecurity. That's not a sign that something is going wrong. That's a sign that the stripping is working. God doesn't use the wilderness to punish His people. He uses it to reveal Himself to them in a way that Egypt's noise made impossible.

The path this book traces moves through three distinct territories. The first is recognition: seeing clearly what Egypt has built in you and naming it without flinching. The second is departure: actually creating the distance, making the changes, dismantling the idols one by one with specific and honest action. The third is transformation: discovering what grows in the space those idols used to occupy, and learning what it means to live as a person whose entire life is oriented toward God.

That third territory is where resurrection language becomes appropriate. Because what this process produces isn't just a cleaned-up version of the old life. It's genuinely new. Paul describes it in Romans 6 as dying to one way of living and rising to another. The old patterns don't just get adjusted. They get buried. And what comes up from that burial is a faith that's actually alive, actually different, actually capable of the kind of witness that makes people ask questions they wouldn't otherwise think to ask.

The chapters ahead will cover specific ground. You'll work through materialism and what it's actually cost your spiritual life. You'll look at entertainment and digital culture with honest eyes. You'll examine the worship culture you've inherited and ask whether it's producing transformation or just emotion. You'll look at end-times fear, political entanglement, and the ways the church has sometimes traded its prophetic voice for cultural relevance. Each of these is a brick in the Egyptian system. Each one needs to be examined. Some need to be left behind entirely. Others need to be redeemed and reoriented.

None of this is easy. Anyone who tells you that following God's call to "come out" is painless isn't telling you the truth. Abraham left his country, his family, and his father's house. That cost something real.

Israel walked into a wilderness with no map and no guarantee except God's word. That required something real. The call this book carries is no different. It's costly. It's specific. And it's the most alive you will ever feel.

What God is asking is significant. What He's offering in return is worth every step of the distance between here and there.

You picked up this book because something in you recognized the gap. Something in you knew that the faith you profess and the life you're living aren't as close as they should be. That recognition is itself a grace. It's God's voice doing what it's always done, from Abraham's tent to Moses at the burning bush to a voice in Revelation cutting through the noise of Babylon: come out. There's something better waiting on the other side of your departure.

1

THE THREE DAYS' JOURNEY

Moses didn't walk into Pharaoh's throne room with a vague request. He came with a number. Three days. That specific detail is easy to read past, but it carries more weight than most people realize. God didn't ask for a short walk to the edge of town. He didn't ask for a day trip that would let Israel be back in their Egyptian homes by nightfall. He asked for three days into the wilderness. Far enough that turning back would be a real decision, not just a short stroll in the other direction.

That distance was the point.

Understanding why God set that specific condition changes how you read the entire Exodus story. And it changes how you read your own life as a believer trying to figure out what genuine faithfulness actually looks like in a world that's constantly pressing you to stay comfortable, stay close, and stay manageable.

The Pattern of Definitive Break

In the ancient world, three days of travel from a major city like Egypt's capital wasn't just a long walk. It placed you completely outside the reach of Egyptian authority, Egyptian supply lines, and Egyptian religious influence. The gods of Egypt were territorial. Their power was understood to operate within Egyptian borders. A three-day journey didn't just create physical distance. It created a different kind of space entirely, one where Egypt's gods had no claim and Egypt's Pharaoh had no jurisdiction. That was exactly what God was after. Not a partial separation. A complete one.

In Jewish thought, three days carried a very specific meaning. A person was considered truly dead after three days. Before that, there was still some hope of resuscitation, some possibility of reversal. After three days, the matter was settled. That's why Jesus deliberately waited until Lazarus had been in the tomb four days before going to Bethany (John 11:17). He wasn't late. He was making a theological statement. He waited past the point of no return so that when Lazarus walked out of that tomb, no one could explain it away as a near-death recovery. It was pure resurrection. Death had been final. And then it wasn't.

This is the symbolic weight the number three carries all through Scripture. One day is a pause. Two days is a delay. Three days is finality. It's the signal that something has ended completely, and whatever comes next is genuinely new.

The pattern shows up so consistently across the Bible that it's clearly not coincidence. Abraham traveled three days to reach Mount Moriah, where he was prepared to sacrifice his son Isaac (Genesis 22:4). Hebrews 11:19 interprets that journey as a figurative resurrection, because Abraham received Isaac back as though from the dead. Jonah spent three days in the belly of the great fish, and Jesus himself pointed to that as a direct picture of His own burial and resurrection (Matthew 12:40). Esther called a three-day fast before she approached the king to plead for her people's lives (Esther 4:16), dying to her own safety and comfort before stepping into the most important moment of her life. Each of these stories follows the same shape: a period of complete separation, a kind of death, and then something new on the other side.

The three-day journey Israel requested from Pharaoh fits this same shape exactly. It wasn't just a logistical requirement. It was a death. A death to the Egyptian identity they'd been living inside for four hundred years. A death to the rhythms, the structures, the habits of mind that slavery had formed in them. You don't shed four centuries of cultural conditioning in an afternoon. You need enough distance that the old world can no longer reach you, and the new world hasn't fully formed around you yet. You need the wilderness in between.

Think about what that means for you personally. The habits and values that culture has built into you over decades don't loosen their grip with a Sunday sermon and a few good intentions. A partial separation, where you keep most of your old patterns intact and just add some spiritual activity on top, doesn't produce transformation. It produces exhaustion. You end up trying to maintain two incompatible lives simultaneously, which is exactly why so many sincere believers feel the gap between their Sunday faith and their Monday reality but can't seem to close it. The gap exists because the break was never complete enough.

Consider someone like Danielle, a hypothetical 34-year-old marketing manager who genuinely loves God and has been in church her whole life. She reads her Bible most mornings, tithes faithfully, and serves in her church's women's ministry. But her financial decisions are driven almost entirely by comparison with her colleagues. She upgraded her car last year not because she needed to but because her coworker's car made her feel behind. She checks her phone within the first five minutes of waking up every single day. She hasn't sat in silence before God for longer than three minutes in years, because the moment the noise stops, the anxiety starts and it feels easier to just keep the noise going. She's not walking away from her faith. She's just never traveled far enough from Egypt for Egypt to stop shaping her. She's worshipping at the edge of the border, with one foot still inside Pharaoh's territory.

The three-day journey calls for something more complete than that. It calls for the kind of break that can't easily be reversed. Not because God is harsh, but because genuine transformation requires enough distance from the old system that you actually have to depend on something different. When Egypt is still within walking distance, you'll walk back to it the moment things get uncomfortable. And things always get uncomfortable when you start letting God change you.

This is also where the resurrection hope lives. The three-day pattern isn't just about death. It's always about what comes after. Abraham got Isaac back. Jonah got a second chance and a whole city got saved. Esther's fast preceded the salvation of an entire people. And Jesus walked out of the tomb. The complete break isn't the end of the story. It's the condition that makes the new story possible. You can't experience resurrection life while you're still refusing to let the old life die.

Pharaoh's Four Compromises

Pharaoh didn't say no every time. That's what makes his responses so worth studying. He negotiated. He offered alternatives. He tried to find a version of Israel's request that he could live with, one that would satisfy their religious needs without actually costing him control over them. And every single offer he made was designed to keep Israel close enough that Egypt still had a claim on them.

The first offer came in Exodus 8:25. Pharaoh said, "Go, sacrifice to your God in the land." Stay in Egypt. Worship here. Keep your faith, but keep it within the system I control. Don't let it take you anywhere I can't follow. This is the most direct form of the compromise, and it's the one that's easiest to recognize. It's the version of Christianity that fits neatly inside the surrounding culture without disturbing anything. You can have your faith as long as it stays in its lane, as long as it doesn't challenge your career ambitions or your spending habits or your entertainment choices or your political identity. Worship in the land. Just don't let it take you anywhere inconvenient.

The second offer came just three verses later in Exodus 8:28. When Moses rejected the first offer, Pharaoh tried again: "I will let you go... only you shall not go very far away." This one is subtler and more dangerous than the first. He's no longer asking them to stay in Egypt. He's just asking them not to go too far. Keep it moderate. Don't be one of those Christians who takes this stuff to an extreme. A little separation is fine. Just don't let it become your whole identity. Don't let it cost you anything significant. Stay close enough that you can come back quickly if you need to.

This is the compromise that catches the most sincere believers. They've rejected the obvious version of accommodation. They know they shouldn't just blend in completely. But they've accepted a version of faithfulness that keeps them just close enough to Egypt that their lives don't look particularly different from anyone else's. They fast occasionally but never long enough to feel it. They give generously but never enough to change their lifestyle. They stand for truth in comfortable conversations but go quiet when it costs something real. Not far away. Just not very far.

The third compromise Pharaoh offered involved the children. In Exodus 10:10-11, he told Moses that the men could go, but the children had to stay. This is one of the most devastating compromises because it targets the next generation. You can have your personal faith. You can even practice it with some real commitment. But don't raise your children in it. Don't let your faith shape their education, their values, their understanding of money and success and purpose. Let them grow up inside Egypt's value system and make their own choices when they're older. This is the logic behind handing children over to be formed entirely by a culture that doesn't share your values, and then hoping a Sunday school hour will counterbalance forty hours of contrary formation every week.

The fourth compromise targeted the livestock. In Exodus 10:24, Pharaoh said the people could go, and their children could go, but their flocks and herds had to stay behind. Take your family. Take your faith. But leave your resources under my control. This is the version of the compromise that shows up most clearly in how Christians handle money. You can worship freely as long as your financial decisions are still driven by the same values as everyone else. Keep your career goals, your investment strategy, your spending patterns inside Egypt's logic. Let your resources stay under the world's system even while you claim your heart belongs to God.

What's striking about all four of these offers is how reasonable they sound. None of them are asking Israel to stop believing in God. None of them are asking for outright apostasy. They're just asking for a version of faith that doesn't require a complete break. A faith that stays within manageable limits. A faith that costs something, maybe, but not everything.

Moses rejected every single one. Not because he was inflexible or extreme, but because he understood that partial separation isn't separation at all. It's just a more comfortable form of bondage. If Pharaoh still controls your children, he still controls your future. If he still controls your livestock, he still controls your livelihood. If you stay in the land, you're still under his authority regardless of what you call your religious practice. The compromises weren't generous offers. They were traps dressed up as concessions.

The enemy uses the same four strategies today, and they work for the same reason they worked on Israel: they feel reasonable. They feel like the mature, balanced, non-fanatical approach to faith. The person who keeps their faith private at work so as not to seem strange, who lets their kids absorb whatever the culture teaches and trusts it'll sort itself out, who makes financial decisions based entirely on market logic and calls it wisdom, who never lets their beliefs take them anywhere that makes other people uncomfortable, that person isn't being reasonable. They're accepting Pharaoh's deal. And they're wondering why their faith feels hollow.

The Totality of the Offering

When Pharaoh made his fourth compromise and told Moses to leave the livestock behind, Moses gave an answer that cuts right to the heart of what genuine surrender looks like. In Exodus 10:25-26, Moses said, "You must also give us sacrifices and burnt offerings, that we may sacrifice to the Lord our God. Our livestock also shall go with us; not a hoof shall be left behind. For we must take some of them to serve the Lord our God, and even we do not know with what we will serve the Lord until we arrive there."

Read that last sentence again slowly. "We do not know with what we will serve the Lord until we arrive there."

Moses didn't know exactly what God was going to require. He hadn't received a detailed sacrificial schedule. He didn't have a list of which animals would be needed and which could safely be left in

Egypt. He just knew that everything had to come, because he couldn't predetermine what God would ask for until they were actually in the place of worship. So the only safe position was to bring everything and let God decide at the altar what would be offered there.

That's a remarkable posture. And it's completely opposite to how most people approach their relationship with God. The default approach is to decide in advance what you're willing to give and then present that offer to God. You're willing to give your Sunday mornings. You're willing to give a portion of your income. You're willing to give some of your time and some of your energy and some of your attention. But the career stays off the table. The lifestyle stays off the table. The comfort stays off the table. You've pre-negotiated the terms before you've even arrived at the altar.

Moses refused to do that. Not a hoof shall be left behind. Everything comes. God decides what gets offered. That's the posture of someone who has genuinely left Egypt, because Egypt is the place where you negotiate with God from a position of self-protection. The wilderness is the place where you arrive with everything you have and trust God to be the one who determines what the offering looks like.

This is what makes "blank check" obedience so different from the managed, compartmentalized faith that most believers are actually living. A blank check means you've signed your name at the bottom and left the amount for God to fill in. You've said yes before you know what you're saying yes to. That sounds frightening until you remember who's holding the pen. The God who asks for everything is the same God who provided a ram in the thicket for Abraham, who brought Jonah out of the deep, who raised His own Son from the dead. He doesn't ask for everything because He wants to leave you with nothing. He asks for everything because He knows that the things you're holding back are the very things that are limiting what He can do in you.

The Sinai wilderness wasn't a comfortable place. It had no cities, no markets, no infrastructure, no supply chains. Choosing to go there with all your livestock and your children and your whole community meant choosing to depend on God for everything. Egypt at least had food. Egypt at least had predictability. The wilderness offered neither. What it offered was God. Just God. And for the people who were willing to make that trade, it turned out to be more than enough.

Separation from the world's systems always produces this same experience of fresh dependence. When you stop letting entertainment numb the anxiety, the anxiety surfaces and you have to actually bring it to God. When you stop letting materialism give you the feeling of security, you have to find security somewhere else, and the only place it's actually available is in God's faithfulness. The stripping that happens in the wilderness isn't cruelty. It's God removing the substitutes so that the real thing can take their place. But you can't experience that exchange while you're still keeping one hoof in Egypt.

The totality of the offering is also connected to something else Moses said. He told Pharaoh that they didn't know yet what they would need to sacrifice. That means the offering wasn't primarily about the animals. It was about the posture. God wasn't ultimately after Israel's livestock. He was after their trust. He was after the kind of faith that says, "I don't know what you're going to ask for, but whatever it is, I'm bringing everything so that nothing is unavailable to you." That's the offering God has always been looking for. Not a specific amount. Not a specific act. A specific orientation of the heart that holds nothing back.

Starting Your Own Three-Day Walk

Everything in this chapter has been building toward a practical question: what does your three-day journey actually look like right now, in your specific life, with your specific habits and your specific attachments?

The three-day motif in Scripture is always about a transition from death to life. Something old ends completely. Something new becomes possible. But that transition requires a definitive break, not a gradual fade, not a slow reduction, not a series of small adjustments that never quite add up to a real change. A break. The kind that's clear enough that you can point to it and say, "That's when things changed."

Pharaoh's four compromises are worth reviewing one more time as a personal diagnostic. Ask yourself honestly: which one are you accepting right now? Are you keeping your faith inside the land, private and unthreatening and carefully contained? Are you following God but "not very far," keeping your life close enough to Egypt's values that the distance is comfortable? Are you allowing your children to be formed primarily by a culture that doesn't share your convictions? Are you leaving your financial decisions, your career logic, your spending patterns entirely inside the world's system while calling yourself a follower of Christ?

You don't have to answer all of those questions at once. But you do have to answer them honestly. The compromises are subtle enough that most people have accepted at least one without fully realizing it. Naming which one it is for you is the first real step of the journey.

Below are three specific, concrete actions to begin your own three-day walk this week. These aren't suggestions for someday. They're moves you can make in the next seven days that will create real distance between you and whatever version of Egypt still has a claim on your life.

First: Identify one "Egyptian" habit to cut this week, completely and specifically. Not reduce. Cut. Pick one thing that Egypt has been using to keep you close, one habit that numbs your spiritual sensitivity, drains your time, or reinforces the world's values in your thinking. It might be thirty minutes of social media scrolling before bed. It might be a specific type of entertainment that consistently pulls your mind away from God. It might be checking your investment portfolio every morning as a ritual of finding security. Whatever it is, name it specifically, write it down, and stop it entirely for seven days. Not forever. Just seven days. The goal isn't permanent deprivation. The goal is to create enough distance to see clearly what that habit has been doing to your soul. When you stop it, pay attention to what fills the space. The discomfort you feel is information.

Second: Create one physical boundary that protects a specific block of time for prayer, starting tomorrow morning. Not "I'll try to pray more." A physical boundary. That means your phone stays in another room during that time. It means you sit in a specific chair or a specific spot that becomes associated with meeting God. It means you set a timer for a specific number of minutes, at least fifteen, and you stay in that space for the full time even if the first several minutes feel dry and awkward and unproductive. The point isn't the feeling. The point is the distance. You're creating a space where Egypt can't reach you, where the noise stops and God has room to speak. Do this for seven consecutive days and track what happens. Write down one thing you noticed or heard from God each day, even if it's small.

Third: Do a "hoof inventory" of one area of your life where you've been negotiating the terms of your offering. Pick one category: money, time, relationships, career, or comfort. Write down specifically what you've been keeping off the altar in that category. Not what you've been giving, but what you've been holding back. Then write one sentence that functions as a blank check in that area: "God, in this area, I don't know what you're going to ask for, but I'm bringing everything. You decide what gets offered." You don't have to know what the sacrifice will be. Moses didn't. You just have to bring everything to the journey so that nothing is unavailable to God when you arrive at the place of worship.

These three steps won't complete your three-day journey. They'll start it. And a journey that's started, even imperfectly, is infinitely further along than one that's only been considered. The distance between Egypt and genuine encounter with God is real. It requires real movement. But every step away from the border is a step toward something that no amount of Egyptian comfort has ever been able to give you.

2

GOD'S JUDGMENT ON EGYPT'S GODS

Most people read the ten plagues as a power contest. God versus Pharaoh. The stronger force wins. But that reading misses almost everything that was actually happening in those chapters of Exodus. The plagues weren't a show of raw power. They were a systematic, methodical, targeted dismantling of an entire way of understanding reality. God wasn't just breaking Pharaoh's will. He was breaking Pharaoh's world.

Egypt's religion wasn't a collection of myths people told around fires at night. It was a working explanation for everything. The Nile flooded and receded on a predictable schedule, and that was Hapi, the god of the inundation, keeping the land alive. The sun rose every morning and crossed the sky, and that was Ra, the greatest of the gods, making his daily journey. Frogs swarmed the riverbanks and were seen as symbols of fertility and new life, connected to the goddess Heqet. Cattle were sacred, tied to the goddess Hathor. The land's productivity, the health of its people, the authority of its Pharaoh, all of it was woven together into one coherent religious system that explained why Egypt was the greatest civilization on earth and why its gods deserved worship.

Then God started pulling that system apart, one thread at a time.

Deconstructing the Worldview

The first plague turned the Nile to blood. That wasn't just an ecological disaster. It was a direct strike against Hapi, the god of the Nile, and against Osiris, whose bloodstream the Nile was believed to be. The most sacred, life-giving force in Egypt's world became death. The thing they trusted most became the thing that couldn't sustain them. Fish died. The water stank. The Egyptians couldn't drink from it. And the god they credited with providing all of it was silent.

The second plague brought frogs. Everywhere. Out of the same Nile that had just been turned to blood. And here's the piece most people miss: frogs were sacred in Egypt. Heqet, the goddess of fertility and childbirth, was depicted with a frog's head. The Egyptians wouldn't kill a frog any more than they'd slap a priest. So when frogs swarmed every home, every bed, every oven and kneading bowl, they couldn't even get rid of them without violating their own religious convictions. Their own sacred symbol had become their torment. God didn't just attack Egypt's gods. He used those gods against their own worshippers.

This pattern keeps going through all ten plagues. Gnats from the dust of the earth, attacking Geb, the god of the earth. Flies swarming everywhere, striking at Khepri, the scarab-headed god. Livestock disease, targeting Hathor and Apis, the sacred bull. Boils, humiliating the Egyptian priests who were supposed to stand before Pharaoh as representatives of divine power but couldn't even stand up because of the sores covering their bodies. Hail destroying the crops, attacking Nut, the sky goddess, and Osiris, god of vegetation. Locusts consuming what the hail left behind. Darkness covering the land for three days, silencing Ra himself, the sun god who was considered the supreme deity of all Egypt. And finally, the death of the firstborn, striking at Pharaoh himself, who was considered a god in human form, the living son of Ra.

Ten plagues. Ten domains of Egyptian life and religion. Not one of them random.

This is the part that should stop you. God didn't attack Egypt. He attacked Egypt's gods. He moved through every category of Egyptian existence, every area where Egypt had placed its trust, and He showed, one by one, that none of those things could deliver what Egypt believed they could. The Nile can't give life when God says otherwise. The sun can't shine when God says otherwise. The earth can't produce when God says otherwise. Pharaoh himself can't protect his own household when God says otherwise.

The question that this raises for you isn't historical. It's personal. Every person builds a framework for understanding life. A set of things they trust to provide security, meaning, identity, and order. For Egypt, those things had names and temples. For most people today, they don't look religious at all, which makes them harder to see clearly. But they function exactly the same way. They're the things you trust to explain your life and hold it together when things get hard.

Think about what that framework actually looks like for most Christians living in Western culture right now. Financial stability is trusted to provide security. Career success is trusted to provide identity and significance. Health is trusted to provide a sense of control over the future. Relationships are trusted to provide belonging and emotional safety. Entertainment and stimulation are trusted to provide relief from anxiety and a sense that life is worth living. None of these things are inherently evil. But when they become the load-bearing walls of your life, the things that would cause everything to collapse if they were removed, they've become something more than good gifts.

They've become gods. And God has a long history of sending plagues against gods.

The escalating nature of the ten plagues is worth sitting with carefully. They didn't start with the death of the firstborn. They started with something inconvenient. A river turned to blood is a serious problem, but you can dig wells beside the Nile and find water. You can manage. It's uncomfortable, but it's survivable. Then frogs. Then gnats. Then flies. Each plague was more disruptive than the last, moving from the inconvenient to the devastating, from the natural world to the human body, and finally to life and death itself. That escalation wasn't accidental. It mirrors exactly how God tends to work when He's dealing with idolatry in a person's life.

He starts gently. A small disruption. A nagging sense that the thing you've been trusting isn't as reliable as you thought. A financial setback that's uncomfortable but manageable. A relationship that disappoints you in a way that exposes how much weight you'd placed on it. A health scare that passes but leaves you shaken. Most people at this stage make adjustments and keep going. They don't stop to ask what God might be saying through the disruption. They just find another well to dig beside the Nile.

When the gentle exposure doesn't produce a response, the disruption increases. The inconvenience becomes a crisis. The manageable problem becomes something you can't manage your way out of. This isn't God being cruel. It's God being persistent. He's after something specific: the reorientation of your trust. He wants you to stop looking to the Nile and start looking to Him. And He'll keep turning up the pressure on the Nile until the Nile has been so thoroughly exposed as unreliable that you stop going back to it.

Pharaoh's response to the plagues is one of the most sobering portraits in all of Scripture. After the first plague, he hardened his heart and went back into his palace. After the second, he asked Moses to pray and promised to let the people go, but when the frogs died, he hardened his heart again. This pattern repeated itself through plague after plague. Relief came, and Pharaoh went back to his previous position. The text alternates between saying Pharaoh hardened his own heart and saying God hardened it. Both are true, and together they describe something theologically important: repeated resistance to God's revelation doesn't just leave you where you started. It moves you backward. Each time Pharaoh chose to harden himself, the next hardening came more easily. What started as a choice eventually became a condition. What once felt like a decision eventually felt like his nature.

This is what prolonged accommodation to idols does to a person. It doesn't just leave you spiritually stagnant. It calcifies you. The first time you chose comfort over obedience, it felt like a choice. The tenth time, it felt like wisdom. The hundredth time, it feels like just who you are. The compromise that once pricked your conscience now feels completely normal, even virtuous. You've rationalized it so many times that the rationalization has become your theology. And by that point, the hardening has become judicial. God isn't just watching you resist Him. He's allowing the consequences of that resistance to set in ways that become increasingly difficult to reverse.

Consider someone like Thomas, a hypothetical 47-year-old who grew up in a strong Christian home and genuinely committed his life to Christ in his twenties. Over the years, the demands of building a career and raising a family slowly pushed his prayer life to the margins. He still went to church. He still gave. But his daily decisions were driven almost entirely by financial logic and social comparison. When a mentor once gently suggested his lifestyle might be outpacing his values, Thomas felt a real sting of conviction. He prayed about it for a week. Then things got busy, and the feeling faded. Five years later, the same observation from a different person produced almost no reaction at all. Not because Thomas had rejected God. But because the heart that was once sensitive to that kind of challenge had slowly hardened through years of choosing not to respond. What once felt like a warning now just felt like someone else's opinion. That's not a dramatic fall. That's how calcification works. Quietly. Gradually. Until what once moved you doesn't move you anymore.

The good news in this picture, and there is good news, is that God's judgments against Egypt were not indiscriminate. Starting with the fourth plague, the text makes an explicit distinction that changes everything. In Exodus 8:22-23, God told Moses that the land of Goshen, where Israel lived, would be set apart. No flies there. While all of Egypt swarmed, Goshen was still. God said, "I will put a division between My people and your people." The same God who sent the plagues also drew a line around His people and said, "Not here. Not them."

That distinction held through every subsequent plague. When the livestock of Egypt died, Israel's livestock lived. When hail destroyed Egypt's fields, Goshen's fields were untouched. When darkness covered the land for three days, Israel had light in their homes. God wasn't judging indiscriminately. He was judging specifically, targeting the gods of Egypt while protecting the people who belonged to Him. His judgments were redemptive, not random. They were surgical, not scattered.

This matters enormously for how you read the disruptions in your own life. When God sends circumstances that expose the emptiness of what you've been trusting, He isn't targeting you with punishment. He's targeting the idol. He's going after the thing that has taken His place in your life, and He's doing it because He loves you enough to refuse to share you with something that can't actually hold you. The plague falls on the false god, not on the person who belongs to Him. The distinction God drew at Goshen is the same distinction He draws around His people today. The disruption is mercy. The exposure is love. The stripping away of the false thing is the precondition for receiving the real thing.

A financial downturn that reveals how much of your sense of security was built on your bank account rather than God's faithfulness isn't punishment. It's God doing to your idol of wealth exactly what He did to Hapi when He turned the Nile to blood. A health crisis that exposes how much of your sense of control was built on self-sufficiency rather than dependence on God isn't abandonment. It's God doing to your idol of self-reliance what He did to the Egyptian priests when He covered them with boils they couldn't cure. A cultural shift that strips away the social prestige your faith once carried isn't a sign that God has forgotten the church. It's God doing to the idol of respectability what He did to Ra when He covered Egypt in darkness for three days.

The plagues didn't fall because God was angry with Egypt's people in some general, undifferentiated way. They fell because Egypt's gods were lies, and those lies were holding people in a system that couldn't give them what they actually needed. God's judgment against those gods was, in the deepest sense, an act of liberation. He was clearing the ground. He was showing, in terms that couldn't be argued with, that the things Egypt had built its world on were empty. And He was doing it so that when Israel left, they left with no lingering temptation to wonder whether Egypt's gods might have had something to offer after all. By the time the plagues were finished, Egypt's entire religious system had been exposed as powerless. There was nothing left to go back to.

That's what God is after when He sends disruption into your life. Not your suffering. Your freedom. He wants to expose the idols so thoroughly, so unmistakably, that when He calls you forward, you leave with nothing pulling you back. The plague on the Nile was mercy. The darkness over Egypt was mercy. The death of the firstborn was the final, devastating mercy that broke Pharaoh's grip and set Israel free. None of it felt like mercy while it was happening. But on the other side of it, a whole people walked out of slavery into the wilderness, and not one of them was wondering whether Hapi might still have something to offer.

The Mercy of Disruption

The word "mercy" and the word "crisis" don't usually appear in the same sentence. When something in your life breaks down, mercy isn't the first word that comes to mind. Loss feels like loss. Disruption feels like disruption. The experience of having something you depended on suddenly stop working doesn't produce gratitude in the moment. It produces panic, grief, and the desperate search for a way to get back to what you had before.

But the Exodus story insists on something that cuts against that instinct. It insists that the most loving thing God can do for a person who has built their life on a false foundation is to let that foundation fail. Not because He enjoys watching people suffer, but because a false foundation that holds is more dangerous than a false foundation that collapses. If the Nile had kept flowing normally, Egypt would have kept worshipping Hapi. If the livestock had stayed healthy, Egypt would have kept bowing to Hathor. If the sun had kept rising on schedule, Ra would have continued to receive the worship that belongs only to God. The plagues were mercy precisely because they refused to let the lies hold.

The same logic applies to your life with uncomfortable directness. The idol that's working is the idol you'll never question. The marriage that makes you feel complete will never prompt you to ask whether you've made your spouse carry a weight that only God can carry, until the marriage goes through a season that it can't carry. The career that's going well will never prompt you to examine whether your identity is built on your performance rather than on who God says you are, until the career hits a wall. The financial cushion that feels adequate will never force you to confront whether your peace is built on your savings account rather than on God's provision, until the cushion shrinks faster than you expected.

God is not the author of evil, and He doesn't manufacture suffering for its own sake. But He is sovereign over every circumstance, and He is committed enough to your freedom that He'll allow the idols to be exposed rather than let them keep holding you in a comfortable bondage. That's not a small distinction. It's the difference between a God who is indifferent to your spiritual condition and a God who loves you enough to refuse to leave you in it.

The mercy of disruption works in a specific sequence. First, the disruption exposes what you've been trusting. When the thing you depended on stops working, you find out very quickly how much weight you'd placed on it. This is the diagnostic function of crisis. It doesn't create your idols. It reveals them. The anxiety that floods in when your financial security is threatened tells you something about where your security was actually located. The despair that follows a broken relationship tells you something about how much of your identity was wrapped up in that relationship. The spiritual numbness that surfaces when you take away entertainment tells you something about how much you'd been using it to manage your inner life rather than bringing that inner life to God.

Second, the disruption creates an opening. When the thing that was filling the space is removed, there's suddenly room for something else. This is the part that most people miss because they spend all their energy trying to get the old thing back rather than paying attention to what God might be offering in the space it left. Israel stood at the edge of the Red Sea with Egypt behind them and nothing but water in front of them, and their instinct was to turn around and go back. But the opening that felt like a dead end was actually the moment right before the miracle. The disruption had done its work. The idol was behind them. And God was about to do something in the open space that Egypt could never have produced.

Third, the disruption invites a specific response. Not just emotional processing. Not just grief. A reorientation of trust. This is where the mercy becomes actionable. The question the disruption is always asking is: will you put your weight on Me now? Will you let what failed show you what was always true, that I was the only foundation that was ever actually load-bearing? The response God is looking for isn't stoic acceptance of loss. It's active, specific, deliberate transfer of trust from the thing that failed to the God who hasn't.

This is also where the distinction between Israel and Egypt becomes personally significant. Both groups experienced the plagues. But they experienced them completely differently. For Egypt, the plagues were pure destruction. For Israel, they were the mechanism of liberation. The same events. Completely different meanings, depending on whose side of the Goshen line you were standing on. When God's people go through disruption, it's not the same experience as when people without God go through disruption. The circumstances might look identical from the outside. But the person who belongs to God is going through a stripping that leads somewhere. The darkness isn't the end of the story. It's the three days before the morning.

Most Christians intellectually agree with this. They know God is sovereign. They know He works all things together for good. They can quote Romans 8:28 from memory. But in the actual experience of disruption, that knowledge stays abstract. It's a comfort they hold in their minds without it reaching the place where the fear lives. The gap between knowing it and feeling it is real, and it's worth being honest about.

The way that gap closes isn't through more information. It's through practice. Specifically, through the practice of interpreting disruption through a biblical lens in real time, while it's happening, rather than only in retrospect. This means that when something fails, the first question you train yourself to ask isn't "how do I fix this?" but "what is this exposing?" That's a hard discipline to build. It goes against every instinct. But it's the discipline that turns disruption into revelation instead of just loss.

It's also worth being clear about what this doesn't mean. Saying that God uses disruption as mercy doesn't mean every hard thing is a plague against a specific idol. Sometimes things are just hard. Sometimes loss is just loss, and the most faithful response is grief, not immediate spiritual analysis. The point isn't to turn every difficulty into a theological puzzle to solve. The point is to hold disruption with open hands rather than clenched fists, staying available to what God might be doing in it rather than spending all your energy resisting it.

The Israelites who watched the plagues fall on Egypt while Goshen stayed untouched were learning something they'd need for the wilderness ahead. They were learning that God's protection doesn't mean the absence of difficulty. It means the presence of God in the middle of it. They weren't insulated from the chaos around them. They were distinguished within it. And that distinction was itself a form of testimony. When the Egyptians saw that the flies weren't in Goshen, when they saw that Israel's livestock were alive while Egypt's were dead, they were seeing something they couldn't explain within their own religious system. God's protection of His people wasn't just for Israel's sake. It was a declaration to Egypt that there was a God whose power operated by completely different rules than the ones Egypt had built its world on.

Your response to disruption carries the same potential. When the people around you are undone by the same circumstances that you're walking through with peace, that's not just personally helpful. It's a witness. Not a performance of false peace, where you pretend things aren't hard. But genuine stability that comes from having your trust located somewhere that the disruption can't reach. That's what the Goshen distinction looked like in practice. Not that Israel had no problems. But that their God was present in the problems in a way that Egypt's gods weren't. And that presence made all the difference.

Putting It Into Practice

This chapter has covered a lot of theological ground, but theology that doesn't land in your actual life this week isn't doing its full work. The plagues were specific. God's targets were specific. The distinction He drew at Goshen was specific. The response He was looking for from both Egypt and Israel was specific. Your response to this chapter should be specific too.

What follows are four concrete actions. They're designed to work together, and they build on each other. Work through them in order over the next two weeks.

First: Perform an idol audit on your current anxieties. Get a piece of paper and write down the top three things that produce the most anxiety in your life right now. Not vague worries, but specific ones. Your financial situation. Your health or someone you love's health. A relationship that feels unstable. Your career trajectory. Your children's choices. Now, for each one, write this question beside it: "If this were taken away entirely, what would I lose that I'm currently getting from it?" Security? Identity? A sense of control? Belonging? The answer to that question tells you what the thing has been providing that you haven't been getting from God. That's the idol. You're not looking for something dramatic or obviously sinful. You're looking for the functional god, the thing that's been doing for you what only God should be doing. Name it clearly. Write the name beside each anxiety. This audit takes thirty minutes and it's one of the most honest things you can do for your spiritual life right now.

Second: Identify which "plague" God may already be sending against one of those idols. Look at the three idols you named. Is there already a disruption happening in one of those areas? A financial pressure that won't resolve? A health situation that keeps surfacing? A relationship that keeps disappointing you in the same way? If so, stop trying to fix it for one week. Instead, ask God specifically: "What are you exposing here? What have I been trusting in this area that I should have been trusting you for?" Write down whatever comes to mind when you sit quietly with that question for ten minutes each day. You're not looking for a dramatic revelation. You're looking for an honest answer. Even a partial one is enough to work with.

Third: Choose one specific area of trust to actively transfer to God this week. Based on what the audit revealed, pick one area where you've been trusting something other than God for something only God can provide. Then take one concrete action that reflects a transfer of trust in that area. If it's financial anxiety, give away a specific amount of money that feels slightly uncomfortable, not to the point of irresponsibility, but enough that it requires you to trust God's provision rather than your own management. If it's the idol of health and self-sufficiency, schedule one day where you deliberately don't check the symptoms you've been researching, and instead spend that time praying specifically about your body and your mortality. If it's a relationship idol, have one honest conversation with that person where you stop managing their impression of you and just tell the truth. The action should be specific enough that you can describe it in one sentence and concrete enough that someone else could verify you did it.

Fourth: Repent specifically, not generally. Repentance that stays vague stays ineffective. After the idol audit, take five minutes to pray through each idol you named with this specific structure: name the idol out loud, name what you've been getting from it that you should have been getting from God, and ask God specifically to become that thing for you. If wealth has been your security, say that. "God, I've been getting my sense of safety from my savings account rather than from your faithfulness. I repent of that specifically. I'm asking you to be my security." If entertainment has been your relief from anxiety, say that. "God, I've been using entertainment to manage the anxiety that I should have been bringing to you. I repent of that specifically. I'm asking you to be my peace." This kind of specific repentance does something that general confession can't do. It names the exact place where the transfer of trust needs to happen, which makes it possible for you to actually notice when it starts happening.

God's judgment on Egypt's gods wasn't the end of the story. It was the beginning of Israel's freedom. The plagues cleared the ground. They exposed the lies. They broke the grip of the system that had held God's people in bondage for four hundred years. And when the last plague fell and Pharaoh finally released them, Israel walked out of Egypt into a wilderness that had no Nile, no Ra, no Hapi, no Hathor. Just God. And that turned out to be exactly enough.

The same God who drew a line around Goshen draws a line around you. The same God who targeted Egypt's gods with surgical precision knows exactly which idols in your life need to be exposed. The disruptions you've been trying to manage your way out of may be the most targeted acts of mercy God has ever shown you. The question isn't whether He's at work in them. The question is whether you're willing to stop going back to the Nile long enough to find out what He's offering instead.

3

BABYLON

There's a voice that cuts through the noise of Revelation 18 like nothing else in the chapter. Cities are falling. Merchants are weeping. Kings who built their power on a corrupt system are watching it collapse in a single hour. And right in the middle of all that chaos, a voice from heaven speaks four words that God has been saying in one form or another since the beginning of human history: "Come out of her, My people."

Four words. But they carry the weight of the entire biblical story behind them.

The "her" in that sentence is Babylon. And if you think Babylon is just an ancient city that fell centuries ago, you've missed the most important thing this chapter has to say. Babylon isn't primarily a place on a map. It's a system. A civilization-level way of organizing human life around everything except genuine dependence on God. And it's been running, in one form or another, since the first bricks were laid at a place called Babel.

The Babylon Thread

Genesis 11 opens with a scene that seems almost innocent at first. A group of people, speaking the same language, decide to build a city with a tower that reaches to heaven. They want to make a name for themselves. They want to stay together, stay unified, stay in control of their own destiny. On the surface, it sounds like ambition. Read a little more carefully, and you see something else entirely.

The tower they were building was a ziggurat. Ancient Near Eastern cultures built these massive stepped structures as meeting points between heaven and earth, places where the gods could descend and humans could ascend. The idea was to reach the divine on human terms, through human engineering, human organization, and human effort. God wasn't invited to define the terms of the encounter. Humanity would build its own staircase to heaven and set the conditions of access. That's the founding idea of Babel. And it's the founding idea of every version of Babylon that follows it through the rest of Scripture.

Babylon is what happens when human civilization decides it can build something that replaces dependence on God.

The thread runs straight from that tower to Nebuchadnezzar's Babylon centuries later. When Nebuchadnezzar built a golden image ninety feet tall and commanded every person in his empire to bow to it at the sound of the music, he wasn't just showing off his power. He was doing what Babylon always does: demanding uniform worship of the state's chosen symbol. The system requires everyone to bow. It can't tolerate people who answer to a higher authority, because people who answer to a higher authority are always a threat to a system built on the premise that there is no higher authority. That's why Shadrach, Meshach, and Abednego ended up in a furnace. Not because Nebuchadnezzar was uniquely cruel. But because Babylon, by its very nature, cannot coexist peacefully with people who won't bow.

Daniel understood this and lived inside it for decades without becoming it. He served in the Babylonian government faithfully. He interpreted dreams for pagan kings. He held high office in the very administration of the empire that had destroyed Jerusalem and carried his people into exile. And yet when the law changed to forbid prayer to anyone but the king, Daniel went home, opened his window toward Jerusalem, and prayed three times a day exactly as he always had. He didn't withdraw from Babylon. He refused to let Babylon define his allegiance. That's a distinction worth holding onto, because it becomes critical later in this chapter.

The prophets saw Babylon clearly for what it was. Isaiah 47 describes it as a nation that said in its heart, "I am, and there is no one else besides me." That sentence is the theological core of Babylon in every generation. It's the declaration of self-sufficiency. The claim that the system is complete without God. Jeremiah 50 and 51 describe its coming judgment in terms so total that nothing is left standing. Not because God is cruel, but because a civilization built on the premise of human self-sufficiency without God has no foundation that can hold forever.

And then Revelation 17 and 18 bring the thread all the way to its end. The Babylon of Revelation isn't a specific modern city. It's the final, fully developed expression of the same system that started at Babel. A civilization of staggering wealth, global influence, cultural dominance, and spiritual corruption. The angel who announces her fall says she "made all the nations drink of the wine of the passion of her immorality." That's not just religious language. That's a description of a system so pervasive, so intoxicating, so thoroughly woven into the fabric of daily life that the nations don't even realize they're drunk on it.

The arc from Babel to Revelation isn't a history lesson. It's a description of the water you're swimming in right now. Every generation has its version of Babylon, the dominant system that organizes life around wealth, power, and cultural influence while offering religious language as a veneer over what is fundamentally a human-centered project. The specific form changes. The underlying structure doesn't.

Isaiah 52:11 says it plainly: "Depart! Depart! Go out from there, touch no unclean thing; go out from the midst of her, be clean, you who bear the vessels of the Lord." God has been saying this to His people across every generation. The call to come out isn't a new idea in Revelation 18. It's the same call Abraham heard in Ur. The same call Moses carried to Pharaoh. The same call the prophets repeated to a people who kept drifting back toward the systems God had called them out of. The voice doesn't change. The system it's calling you out of just changes its clothes in every new era.

The Harlot and the City

Revelation's portrait of Babylon is deliberately two-sided. In chapter 17, Babylon appears as a harlot, a seductive woman dressed in purple and scarlet, drunk with the blood of the saints, sitting on many waters. In chapter 18, she appears as a great city, a commercial powerhouse whose merchants have grown rich from her luxury, whose trade networks span the known world, whose collapse sends the global economy into mourning. Same Babylon. Two faces. And you need both of them to understand what you're actually dealing with.

The harlot represents religious corruption. Not necessarily the obvious kind, where people bow to literal statues. The more dangerous kind, where genuine spiritual language and real religious emotion get attached to a system that is fundamentally organized around something other than God. The harlot is seductive precisely because she looks like something worth pursuing. She offers spiritual experience, community, transcendence, meaning. She just delivers all of it on terms that keep you dependent on the system rather than on God.

Revelation 18:23 uses a word that's easy to pass over. It says Babylon deceived the nations by her "sorcery." The Greek word there is pharmakeia, the same root we get the word "pharmacy" from. It carries the idea of a drug, something that alters your perception of reality, makes you feel things that aren't quite real, keeps you coming back for the next dose. Babylon's sorcery isn't primarily about occult rituals. It's about the intoxicating power of cultural influence, entertainment, marketing, ideology, and spectacle that keeps people in a state of pleasant confusion about what's actually real and what actually matters.

Think about what that looks like in practice. A steady diet of entertainment that keeps your emotional register calibrated to manufactured drama rather than real life. Marketing that is specifically engineered to create dissatisfaction with what you have and desire for what you don't. Social media platforms designed by some of the most brilliant engineers in the world to keep you scrolling, comparing, performing, and consuming in a loop that produces anxiety and numbness in roughly equal measure. These aren't neutral tools. They're pharmakeia. They alter the way you perceive reality, and they do it so gradually and pleasantly that you don't notice the alteration happening.

The great city side of Babylon is the economic engine that makes all of this possible. Revelation 18 lists the cargo of Babylon's merchants in detail: gold, silver, jewels, pearls, fine linen, purple cloth, silk, scarlet cloth, all kinds of scented wood, all kinds of articles of ivory, all kinds of articles of costly wood, bronze, iron and marble, cinnamon, spice, incense, myrrh, frankincense, wine, oil, fine flour, wheat, cattle, sheep, horses, chariots, and finally, "human souls." The list moves from luxury goods down through staple goods and ends with people. That progression is deliberate. A system that begins with luxury ends by treating human beings as commodities. That's where Babylon's economics always go when they run their full course.

Augustine wrote about two cities in a way that cuts right to the heart of this. He said the city of man is built on love of self to the point of contempt for God. The city of God is built on love of God to the point of contempt for self. Two cities. Two organizing loves. Every human heart is a citizen of one or the other. And the city of man doesn't have to look obviously corrupt to be the city of man. It just has to be organized around self at its center, with God somewhere in the supporting cast.

Consumer culture is one of the clearest expressions of the city of man that has ever existed. It's built on a single premise: your desires are the measure of all things, and the purpose of the economy is to serve them. Every advertisement is a small sermon preaching the same gospel: you deserve more, you need more, more will make you more. That gospel is so pervasive, so deeply embedded in the air you breathe, that most Christians have absorbed it without realizing it. They feel its pull in their financial decisions. They feel it in the way they compare their home to their neighbor's. They feel it in the low-level restlessness that surfaces whenever they sit still long enough to notice it.

Debt-driven living is one of the clearest signs of participation in Babylon's economy. When you spend money you don't have to buy things you don't need to impress people you don't particularly like, you're not just making a financial decision. You're making a theological one. You're saying that your sense of adequacy, your identity, your belonging, are things that can be purchased. That's Babylon's logic.

It's the logic of a system that knows it can keep you dependent as long as it can keep you wanting.

Status-oriented ambition works the same way. There's nothing wrong with working hard, developing skills, or building a career. But when the driving question behind your professional life is "how do I look?" rather than "how do I serve?", when the measure of success is where you rank rather than what you've contributed, you're operating inside Babylon's value system regardless of how many Bible verses you have on your office wall.

Consider someone like Marcus, a hypothetical 41-year-old financial advisor who genuinely loves God and leads a small group at his church. He tithes faithfully. He volunteers. He reads his Bible most mornings. But his career decisions are driven almost entirely by income targets and client acquisition numbers. He upgraded his house last year not because his family needed more space but because his income had reached a level where his current house felt embarrassing. He drives a car he can afford but that he chose specifically because of how it reads to the clients he wants to attract. None of this feels like idolatry to him. It feels like being smart, being responsible, being good at his job. But the organizing logic of his financial life is indistinguishable from the organizing logic of someone who has never heard of Jesus. Babylon doesn't require you to abandon your faith. It just requires you to run your life on its terms while keeping your faith as a weekend activity.

The dual nature of Babylon means that "coming out" has to work on both levels simultaneously. You can renounce false doctrine all day long and still be fully embedded in Babylon's economic system. You can have impeccable theology and still be running your life on consumer culture's terms. Spiritual discernment without economic discernment is incomplete. God isn't just interested in what you believe on Sunday. He's interested in what drives your decisions Monday through Saturday. That's where Babylon's real power lives, not in your stated beliefs but in your daily operating logic.

The Jeremiah Balance

The summons to come out of Babylon is not a summons to disappear from the world. This needs to be said clearly, because the history of the church includes plenty of examples of people who heard God's call to separation and responded by building walls, cutting off relationships, withdrawing from civic life, and treating cultural isolation as the highest form of holiness. That's not what Revelation 18:4 is asking for. And it's not what the rest of Scripture models.

Jesus was specific about this in His prayer in John 17:15. He didn't ask the Father to take His followers out of the world. He asked that they be kept from the evil one while remaining in it. The goal was never removal. The goal was distinction within presence. You stay in the world. You just stop being shaped by it.

Jeremiah 29 is one of the most practically useful passages in the entire Bible for Christians trying to figure out what faithful living inside a fallen system actually looks like. God sent a letter to the Jewish exiles in Babylon through Jeremiah, and what He told them is striking. He didn't say, "Resist the Babylonian system at every turn." He didn't say, "Refuse to participate in Babylonian culture." He said: "Build houses and live in them. Plant gardens and eat their produce. Take wives and have sons and daughters... seek the welfare of the city where I have sent you into exile, and pray to the Lord on its behalf, for in its welfare you will find your welfare."

Seek the welfare of the city. Pray for the city. Build a life there. That's not the language of withdrawal. That's the language of engaged, rooted, present faithfulness inside a system that doesn't share your values.

Daniel is the living embodiment of this balance. He served in the Babylonian government under multiple kings across multiple decades. He interpreted dreams, advised rulers, and held administrative authority in the very empire that had destroyed his homeland. He didn't treat his position as a compromise. He treated it as a calling. But he also knew exactly where his lines were. He wouldn't eat the king's food because it would violate his covenant commitments. He wouldn't stop praying when the law changed. He wouldn't bow to Nebuchadnezzar's image. He served Babylon faithfully in everything that didn't require him to violate his allegiance to God, and he refused Babylon's demands in everything that did. That's the balance. Not all or nothing. Faithful engagement with clear lines.

The difference between Daniel and the Israelites who assimilated completely into Babylonian culture isn't that Daniel refused to participate. It's that Daniel maintained an internal orientation that never shifted. His heart was always toward Jerusalem. He prayed with his window open toward the city where God's presence had dwelt. His soul had a direction, a home, a loyalty that Babylon's comforts and Babylon's threats couldn't dislodge. The external participation was real. The internal allegiance was also real. And the two didn't contradict each other because the allegiance was always primary.

This is what "coming out" actually means at its core. It's not primarily about geography or social withdrawal. It's about the reorientation of your deepest loyalty. It's about having an internal "exit strategy" in your heart, a settled conviction that this world's system is not your home, that its values are not your values, that its definitions of success and security and significance are not the definitions you're living by. That conviction then expresses itself in specific, concrete, Spirit-directed choices. But the choices flow from the conviction, not the other way around. You don't become a stranger in Babylon by making a list of things you won't do. You become a stranger in Babylon by being so thoroughly oriented toward God's city that Babylon's offers simply don't have the pull they used to.

The practical shape of this looks different for different people in different seasons. For one person, it means staying in a corporate career but making financial decisions that are completely out of step with their income bracket because they're giving at a level that reflects their actual allegiance. For another, it means being fully present in their neighborhood and their city while refusing to let the neighborhood's social hierarchies determine who they spend time with. For another, it means serving faithfully in local government while maintaining the freedom to vote their conscience and speak their convictions regardless of political pressure. None of these people have withdrawn from the world. All of them have maintained the internal orientation that keeps them from being swallowed by it.

The warning Jeremiah also includes in that same letter is worth noting. He tells the exiles not to listen to the false prophets who were telling them their exile would be short, that Babylon would fall quickly, that they'd be home in no time. Those prophets were offering a comfortable lie. The truth was harder: the exile would last seventy years. A whole generation would live and die in Babylon. And God's instruction wasn't to hold their breath and wait it out. It was to build, plant, marry, have children, and seek the city's welfare. Live fully in the place you're actually in, not in the place you wish you were. That's a word for believers today who are waiting for the culture to change before they start engaging it faithfully. The culture may not change on your timeline. You're still called to seek its welfare right now, in the city you're actually in, in the generation you're actually living in.

The summons is not to isolation. It's to allegiance. And allegiance that's real always shows up in how you live, what you spend, what you refuse, who you serve, and what you're ultimately building toward.

What Leaving Babylon Actually Looks Like

The call in Revelation 18:4 is addressed to "My people." Not to pagans. Not to people who've never heard of God. To people who already belong to Him. That detail is sobering. It means it's entirely possible to be genuinely saved, genuinely loved by God, genuinely part of His family, and still be so embedded in Babylon's system that you need a divine summons to wake up and leave. God doesn't issue the call with condemnation. He issues it with urgency. The tone of Revelation 18:4 isn't "you should be ashamed of yourself." It's "judgment is coming and I love you too much to let you get caught in it."

That's the mercy underneath the command. He's not calling you out because He's angry. He's calling you out because He knows what's coming for the system you're still living inside, and He doesn't want you in the crossfire.

The following four steps are specific and concrete. They're designed to move you from awareness to actual reorientation. Work through them over the next thirty days, one week at a time.

First: Run a "Babylon audit" on your last thirty days of spending. Pull up your bank statements or credit card history for the past month. Go through every purchase and ask one question about each one: was this decision driven by genuine need, genuine generosity, or genuine enjoyment of God's gifts, or was it driven by comparison, status, boredom, anxiety, or the desire to feel adequate? You're not looking to condemn yourself for every latte. You're looking for the pattern underneath the purchases. Write down the three categories where Babylon's logic shows up most consistently in your spending. Name them specifically: "I spent here because I was comparing myself to..." or "I spent here because I was using it to manage the feeling of..." This audit takes about an hour and it's one of the most honest mirrors you can hold up to your actual allegiances. Do it before moving to the next step.

Second: Identify one specific area where you've been participating in Babylon's economy of status or comparison, and make one concrete change this week that reflects a different allegiance. Based on the audit, pick the clearest example. If you've been upgrading things to manage how you look to others, choose one category of your life where you'll deliberately stop upgrading for the next six months and redirect that money to someone with a genuine need. If you've been consuming entertainment at a volume that's functioning as pharmakeia, keeping you pleasantly numb and spiritually dull, cut one specific platform or show entirely for thirty days and replace that time with something that builds your capacity for silence and prayer. The change should be specific enough to name in one sentence and concrete enough that you'll know whether you did it or not.

Third: Identify one place in your life where you've confused withdrawal with holiness, and take one specific step back into engaged presence this week. This is the Jeremiah balance in practice. Is there a neighbor you've been avoiding because their lifestyle makes you uncomfortable? A coworker you've written off? A civic responsibility you've opted out of because the environment feels too secular? Pick one and take one concrete step toward genuine presence. Invite the neighbor to dinner. Have a real conversation with the coworker that isn't about evangelism but just about being human together. Show up to the city council meeting. Seek the welfare of the city. Write down what you're going to do and when you're going to do it before you close this book.

Fourth: Pray for your city specifically and by name, once a day for the next thirty days. Not a vague prayer for "the world." A specific prayer for the actual city or town where you live. Pray for your mayor by name. Pray for the neighborhood you live in by name. Pray for the schools your children or your neighbors' children attend. Pray for the businesses on your street. This is what Jeremiah told the exiles to do, and it does something specific to your heart when you do it consistently. It's very hard to maintain contempt for a place you're praying for. It's very hard to withdraw from a city you're interceding for daily. The prayer reorients your posture from "how do I protect myself from this culture" to "God, what do you want to do in this city and how can I be part of it?" That shift in posture is itself a form of coming out of Babylon, because Babylon's posture is always self-protective and self-referential. The posture of God's city is always outward, always others-oriented, always asking what can be given rather than what can be gained.

The call to come out of Babylon has always been an act of mercy dressed in the clothes of a command. From the moment God spoke to Abraham in Ur to the voice that cuts through the chaos of Revelation 18, God has been saying the same thing to His people in every generation: the system you're living inside cannot give you what I'm offering, and it cannot survive what's coming. Come out. Not to hide. Not to fight. But to live with your allegiance finally, fully, and visibly in the right place.

That kind of life looks different. It spends differently, works differently, rests differently, and serves differently than the life Babylon offers. And that visible difference, lived out in the ordinary details of

Monday through Saturday, is exactly what it means to be a stranger in a culture of compromise.

4

Constantine's Legacy

The year was 312 AD, and a Roman emperor looked up at the sky before battle and reportedly saw a vision. Whether the details of that moment are exactly as history records them is debated. What isn't debated is what happened next. Constantine won the battle, credited the Christian God with his victory, and within a year issued the Edict of Milan, officially ending the persecution of Christians throughout the Roman Empire. After three centuries of being hunted, imprisoned, and killed for their faith, believers across the empire could finally breathe. Churches could be built openly. Worship could happen without fear. The faith that had spread underground through catacombs and whispered prayers was suddenly welcome in the most powerful halls in the world.

It felt like a miracle. It may have been a trap.

That's not a comfortable thing to say about a moment that brought genuine relief to millions of suffering believers. And it's important to be honest: not everything that followed was bad. Hospitals were built. Literacy spread. Legal reforms happened. Scripture was preserved and copied with imperial resources. Christians who had been hiding in the shadows were now free to build, teach, and serve in the open. Those were real goods. They shouldn't be dismissed.

But something else happened too. Something subtler and far more dangerous than the persecution that had just ended. The church stopped being a movement that existed in tension with the surrounding empire and started becoming the empire's spiritual department. The cross, which had been a symbol of shameful execution that the church had transformed into its most powerful image, began appearing on Roman military shields. The faith of a crucified peasant from Galilee became the official religion of the most powerful political machine in the ancient world. And somewhere in that transition, a question got quietly answered in the wrong direction: whose kingdom are we actually building here?

The Cost of Cultural Favor

There's a phrase that captures what happened to the church after Constantine better than almost any other. The church went from being an ambassador of an alternative kingdom to being a chaplain to the empire. Read those two roles side by side and the difference becomes clear immediately. An ambassador represents a foreign power. They live in a country that isn't their home, speak on behalf of a king who isn't the local ruler, and their ultimate loyalty is always to the kingdom they came from, not the kingdom they're stationed in. A chaplain, on the other hand, exists to serve the institution they're embedded in. They provide spiritual comfort and religious legitimacy to the organization's goals. Their role is to bless what the institution is already doing.

That shift from ambassador to chaplain is what scholars sometimes call the Constantinian Trap. And it's not just a fourth-century problem.

The structural pattern is this: whenever the church trades prophetic distance for political proximity, it gains influence but loses its distinctive voice. It gets a seat at the table. It gets cultural respect. It gets legal protection and social prestige. And in exchange, it gradually stops saying the things that only a church with nothing to lose can say. The prophetic edge softens. The willingness to speak truth to power fades. The church begins to define its mission as maintaining the culture's Christian character rather than proclaiming a crucified and risen King whose kingdom operates by completely different rules than the ones the culture runs on.

The church at Pergamum in Revelation 2 is worth pausing on here. Jesus described that church as dwelling "where Satan's throne is." Pergamum was a major center of Roman imperial cult worship. The pressure to accommodate, to blend in, to find a version of Christianity that didn't put you in conflict with the dominant culture, was enormous there. And the church at Pergamum compromised. They allowed false teaching to take root. They ate food sacrificed to idols. They tolerated what they should have rejected. Not because they stopped believing in Jesus, but because the social cost of full faithfulness was higher than they were willing to pay. They wanted to stay in good standing with the city. They wanted to be respected. They wanted legitimacy. And the price of that legitimacy was their prophetic sharpness.

That's the Constantinian Trap in miniature. The pressure to be acceptable, to be respected, to be welcomed by the surrounding culture, is powerful enough to reshape what the church says, what it's willing to challenge, and who it's ultimately serving. When cultural favor becomes something the church is trying to protect, the church has already lost something it can't afford to lose.

The Anabaptists understood this. In the sixteenth century, when the mainstream Reformation was still working within the framework of state churches, a group of believers in Zurich made a radical decision. They rejected the idea that the church's identity should be tied to the political structure of any nation or city. They insisted on believer's baptism, meaning only those who had personally chosen faith should be baptized, rather than infants being baptized into a civic-religious identity. They separated church and state not as a political theory but as a theological conviction: the church is a distinct people with a distinct King, and its authority comes from that King alone, not from any earthly ruler's endorsement. For this, they were persecuted by both Catholics and Protestants. They were drowned, burned, and hunted across Europe.

They paid the price of refusing the Constantinian bargain. And their witness stands as one of the clearest examples in church history of what it looks like to maintain a distinct kingdom identity when the surrounding culture is offering a more comfortable arrangement.

The nationalism question deserves direct attention here, because it's where the Constantinian pattern shows up most visibly in contemporary church life. When a national flag stands alongside the cross in a sanctuary, something theological is being communicated, whether intentionally or not. It's communicating that the identity of God's people and the identity of a particular nation are bound together in some meaningful way. That the church's mission is somehow connected to the nation's success. That being a good Christian and being a good American, or a good citizen of whatever nation you're in, are essentially the same project. Philippians 3:20 cuts through that assumption without apology: "Our citizenship is in heaven." Not as a secondary citizenship that supplements the earthly one. As the primary identity that relativizes every earthly one.

This doesn't mean Christians shouldn't love their country, vote, serve in government, or care about their nation's direction. The Jeremiah balance from the previous chapter applies here too. You can seek the welfare of the city without making the city's success the measure of the church's faithfulness. But the moment the church's sense of security or significance becomes tied to a nation's political health, the Constantinian Trap has been sprung again. The church has become a chaplain to the empire, blessing the flag rather than proclaiming the cross.

The decline of what scholars call "Cultural Christendom" in the West is worth naming directly here, because most Christians experience it as a crisis. For centuries, Western culture carried at least the outward shape of Christian values. Laws reflected Christian ethics. Politicians used Christian language. Churches were culturally central. Being a Christian was, in most social contexts, the respectable and normal thing to be. That world is ending rapidly, and many believers experience its ending as a catastrophic defeat.

It may actually be a liberation.

When the church no longer has cultural prestige to protect, it's free to be what it was always called to be: a minority community of people whose lives are visibly shaped by a different set of values than the surrounding culture. The early church had no cultural prestige. It had no political endorsement. It had no legal protection for its first three centuries. And it turned the ancient world upside down. Not because it held power, but because it embodied something so genuinely different, so visibly other, that people couldn't stop asking what it was. The loss of Christendom's scaffolding might be the thing that forces the church to rediscover what it was always supposed to be standing on.

Consider someone like Pastor James, a hypothetical 52-year-old who leads a mid-sized evangelical church in a suburban community. He's watched his congregation shrink over the past decade as the surrounding culture has become less sympathetic to traditional Christian values. His instinct, shaped by years of thinking inside a Christendom framework, is to respond politically. To mobilize his congregation around candidates and causes that might restore some version of the cultural environment he grew up in. To fight for the church's place at the table. But every time he goes that direction, he notices something: his congregation gets more anxious, more angry, more focused on what they're against, and less focused on who they're for. The political engagement isn't producing the transformation he's hoping for. It's producing a church that's increasingly hard to distinguish from a political action committee with worship music. He's caught in the Constantinian Trap without having a name for it yet.

What James needs, and what the church in this moment needs, isn't a better political strategy. It's a recovered theology of the kingdom. A clear, settled conviction that the church's authority doesn't come from cultural favor, legislative victory, or political proximity. It comes from the Spirit of the living God operating through a people who are genuinely different from the world around them. That's not a retreat from influence. It's the only kind of influence that actually changes people from the inside out.

Jesus made this explicit in John 6:15. When the crowd, having seen His miracles, wanted to take Him by force and make Him king, He withdrew. He didn't leverage the moment. He didn't accept the offer. He walked away from the most obvious political opportunity of His ministry. And later, standing before Pilate, He explained why: "My kingdom is not of this world. If My kingdom were of this world, My servants would fight." The kingdom He came to establish doesn't operate by the world's methods. It doesn't advance through the accumulation of political power. It advances through the cross, the Spirit, and the faithful witness of people who have genuinely died to the world's way of doing things and risen to something different. That's not a weak strategy. It's the only strategy that has ever actually worked.

Paul said it directly in 2 Corinthians 10:3-5. The weapons of our warfare are not carnal. They're not political leverage, cultural dominance, or legislative victory. They're mighty through God for pulling down strongholds. The strongholds Paul has in mind aren't primarily governmental. They're in the mind. They're the arguments and pretensions that set themselves up against the knowledge of God. And those strongholds don't fall to political pressure. They fall to the proclamation of truth, the demonstration of genuine love, and the witness of a community whose life together can't be explained by any merely human motivation.

The Laodicean church in Revelation 3 offers one final image worth sitting with. Jesus described that church as neither hot nor cold, and said He would spit them out of His mouth. What made Laodicea lukewarm wasn't overt apostasy. It was comfort. They were wealthy. They were self-sufficient. They thought they had everything they needed. They said, "I am rich, have become wealthy, and have need of nothing." They didn't know they were wretched, miserable, poor, blind, and naked. Cultural comfort had produced spiritual blindness so complete that they couldn't even see their own condition. That's what the Constantinian Trap ultimately produces in a church that stays inside it long enough. Not dramatic heresy. Just comfortable blindness. A church that has everything the world considers success and has lost the one thing that matters.

The 1 Samuel 8 Parallel

Long before Constantine, God's people made a very similar request. They came to the prophet Samuel with a demand that must have broken his heart to hear: "Give us a king to judge us like all the nations." Samuel was troubled by it. He prayed about it. And God's response to him is one of the most revealing moments in the entire Old Testament. God said, "They have not rejected you, but they have rejected Me, that I should not reign over them."

Read that again. Israel's demand for a king wasn't primarily a political decision. It was a theological one. It was a statement about where their confidence was located. They had watched the nations around them, seen the visible structures of power those nations operated with, kings and armies and clear chains of command, and they'd decided that God's invisible reign wasn't enough. They wanted something they could see. Something that would make them look credible to the surrounding nations. Something that would give them the kind of security and legitimacy that visible power provides.

God told Samuel to warn them about exactly what a king would cost them. He'd take their sons for his army. He'd take their daughters for his household. He'd take the best of their fields and vineyards and olive groves. He'd take a tenth of their grain and their flocks. He'd take their servants and their donkeys. He'd use them for his own purposes. The king they were asking for wouldn't just rule them. He'd consume them. And the day would come when they'd cry out because of the king they'd chosen, and God would not answer.

They asked for him anyway.

The desire for visible, worldly structures of power and legitimacy almost always reflects the same thing it reflected in Israel: a loss of confidence in God's invisible reign. It's not usually a conscious rejection of

God. It's a practical one. It's the quiet conclusion that God's ways are too slow, too unpredictable, too hard to explain to people who want results they can measure and power they can point to. If we just had the right political structures in place. If we just had the right people in the right offices. If we just had enough cultural influence to protect our values. Then we'd be secure. Then we'd be effective. Then we'd matter.

That logic is exactly what Israel said when they asked for a king. And God named it for what it was: a rejection of His reign.

The modern church's version of this request shows up in what might be called "moral majority" thinking. The belief that if enough Christians hold enough political power, society will be transformed. That the right legislation will produce the right culture. That the church's mission is fundamentally about winning elections and appointing judges and passing laws that reflect biblical values. There's nothing wrong with Christians being involved in politics. There's nothing wrong with caring about legislation. But when political victory becomes the primary strategy for the church's mission, something has gone deeply wrong. The transformation God is after doesn't happen through legislative victory. It happens through the cross, the Spirit, and the faithful witness of a people whose lives have genuinely been changed by something no political system can produce.

Israel got their king. And the results were exactly what God warned them about. Saul started well and ended in rebellion and madness. David was a man after God's own heart who committed adultery and orchestrated murder. Solomon, the wisest man who ever lived, ended his life worshipping the gods of his foreign wives. The kingdom split. Then it fell. The very thing they'd demanded as the solution to their insecurity became the source of their greatest catastrophe. The visible structure of power they'd trusted instead of God's invisible reign couldn't hold the weight they'd placed on it.

The parallel to the church's political entanglement isn't subtle. Every time the church has placed its primary confidence in a political figure, a political party, or a legislative agenda, the results have followed the same pattern. The figure disappoints, the party compromises, the legislation gets overturned or proves insufficient, and the church is left having spent enormous energy and credibility on something that couldn't deliver what only God can deliver. Not because politics is evil, but because political power was never designed to carry the weight of the kingdom of God.

There's something else in the 1 Samuel 8 story that's easy to miss. When Samuel prayed about the people's request, God didn't just answer the prayer. He told Samuel to listen to the voice of the people. He allowed them to have what they asked for. That's one of the most sobering forms of divine judgment in Scripture: God giving people what they demand when what they demand is a substitute for Him. He doesn't always prevent the Constantinian bargain. He sometimes lets it run its course so that its inadequacy becomes undeniable. The question is whether the church will learn from that inadequacy or just keep asking for a better king.

The King of Kings is the answer to that question. Not as a slogan. As a settled theological conviction that actually shapes how the church operates, how it measures success, and where it places its confidence. A church that genuinely believes Jesus is King doesn't need cultural prestige to feel secure. It doesn't need legislative victories to feel effective. It doesn't need a seat at the empire's table to feel legitimate. It has something far more solid than any of that: the authority of the risen Christ, operating through the Spirit, in a community of people whose lives are being genuinely transformed. That's not a consolation prize for losing the culture war. That's the actual power of the actual kingdom. And it's more than enough.

The specific danger for believers right now is the version of the 1 Samuel 8 request that's dressed in Christian language. It sounds like this: "We need to take back this nation for God." Or: "If we lose this election, Christianity in America is finished." Or: "The only way to protect our values is to have the right people in power." Every one of those statements, however sincere, places the church's security and effectiveness in the hands of a political outcome rather than in the hands of God. Every one of them is asking for a king like all the nations. And God's response to that request hasn't changed since He gave it to Samuel. He hears it as a rejection of His reign. Not because the people asking it don't love Him, but because the request itself reveals where their confidence is actually located.

The confidence God is looking for is the kind that says, "Whether we win or lose this election, whether this law passes or fails, whether the culture becomes more hostile or more friendly, we know who is King and we know what our job is. Our job is to be a community so genuinely different, so visibly shaped by a different set of values, so clearly operating by a different power, that people can't explain us within the categories the surrounding culture provides." That's the witness that changes things. Not legislation. Not political dominance. A community of people who have genuinely placed their confidence in the invisible reign of a King whose kingdom doesn't depend on any earthly political arrangement to advance.

Putting It Into Practice

The concepts in this chapter carry real weight, but weight that isn't translated into specific action stays abstract. The Constantinian Trap isn't just a historical curiosity. It's a live temptation for every believer trying to figure out how to be faithful in a culture that's rapidly becoming less sympathetic to Christian values. The following steps are designed to help you identify where that trap has already caught you and what to do about it this week.

First: Run a "Constantinian audit" on your political engagement over the past twelve months. This is a specific, honest exercise. Get a piece of paper and write down the five political issues or outcomes you've cared most about in the last year. For each one, write two things beside it. First, how much time, energy, or emotional investment you've given to it. Second, what you were expecting that outcome to produce for your sense of security, your sense of effectiveness as a Christian, or your sense that God's purposes are advancing in the world. Then ask this specific question about each one: "If this issue resolved in exactly the opposite direction from what I want, would I still believe God is King and that His kingdom is advancing?" If the honest answer is no, or even a shaky maybe, you've found a place where the Constantinian Trap has a grip on your thinking. Name it specifically. Write down the exact statement: "I have been placing my confidence in [specific political outcome] rather than in God's reign." That naming is the beginning of the reorientation.

Second: Identify one specific way your church community has functioned as a chaplain to the empire rather than an ambassador of an alternative kingdom. This requires courage and honesty, not condemnation of your church. Look at the past year of your church's public communication, its sermons, its social media, its community conversations. Has the church's posture been primarily shaped by a particular political identity? Has it been more vocal about political enemies than about the gospel? Has it measured its effectiveness by cultural influence rather than by spiritual transformation? Pick one specific example and write it down. Then write what the ambassador posture would have looked like instead. Not a vague improvement, but a specific alternative. "Instead of [specific thing the church did], the ambassador posture would have been [specific alternative]." This exercise isn't about criticizing your church. It's about building your own capacity to recognize the pattern when it appears, so you can pray specifically for your church's leadership and contribute to a different kind of conversation.

Third: Rewrite your personal definition of Christian effectiveness. This is the most important step and it requires the most thought. Take twenty minutes and write out, in your own words, how you currently measure whether your faith is making a difference. Be honest. Most people, if they're honest, will find that their measure of effectiveness is heavily shaped by visible, cultural metrics: how many people agree with their values, whether the political environment is favorable, whether Christianity is respected in their community. Now write a second definition, based specifically on the kingdom Jesus described and modeled. What would effectiveness look like if cultural prestige were completely irrelevant? If political outcomes were completely outside your control? If the only metrics that mattered were spiritual transformation in your own life and genuine love expressed toward the people immediately around you? Write that definition in three to five specific sentences. Then put it somewhere you'll see it every day for the next month, on your phone lock screen, on your bathroom mirror, on a notepad beside your Bible. Read it every morning before you check the news. Let it slowly replace the Constantinian definition with a kingdom one.

Fourth: Choose one specific act of "prophetic distance" from a cultural or political identity you've been too closely attached to. This is the most concrete and the most uncomfortable step. Based on what the Constantinian audit revealed, identify one specific way you've allowed a cultural or political identity to become fused with your Christian identity. It might be a particular political party. It might be a national identity. It might be a media personality or political movement you've treated as a Christian cause. Now take one specific, observable action that creates distance between that identity and your Christian identity. Unfollow one account that has been feeding your sense that political victory is the same as kingdom advancement. Remove one piece of political signaling from a space that's supposed to be about your faith. Have one honest conversation with a fellow believer where you say, "I think I've been too closely tied to [specific political identity] and I'm trying to reorient toward the kingdom." The action should be specific enough that you can describe it in one sentence and concrete enough that you'll know whether you actually did it.

The Constantinian Trap is subtle because it always arrives dressed as responsibility. As caring about the culture. As protecting what matters. As being engaged rather than retreating. None of those motivations are wrong in themselves. The trap springs when the protection of cultural Christianity becomes the goal rather than the proclamation of the actual Christ. When the church starts chaplaining the empire rather than representing the King. When visible structures of power become the basis for the church's confidence rather than the invisible reign of a God who has never once needed a favorable political environment to advance His purposes.

The church was most alive, most distinct, and most genuinely powerful before Constantine offered it legitimacy. That's not nostalgia for persecution. It's an observation about what happens to a community when its security is located in God rather than in cultural favor. That community doesn't need the empire's endorsement. It already has the King's authority. And that turns out to be more than enough to do everything the kingdom actually requires.

5

NOT FAR ENOUGH

Every Christian carries something inherited. A way of doing church. A set of practices that feel sacred not just because Scripture says so, but because your grandmother did them, because your home church always did them, because they've been part of your faith for as long as you can remember. Some of those things are genuinely precious. Some of them are quietly getting in the way. And the hard part is that from the inside, they can feel exactly the same.

This chapter isn't about tearing things down. The goal here is precision, not demolition. It's about recovering the ability to tell the difference between what God actually commanded and what humans added along the way. That distinction matters more than most Christians realize, because the things we've added don't always sit harmlessly beside Scripture. Sometimes they slowly replace it. And when that happens, we end up with a faith that looks busy and feels familiar but isn't producing the transformation God is actually after.

Jesus addressed this directly. He didn't come to abolish tradition as a category. He observed the synagogue system. He celebrated Jewish festivals. He read from the Torah scroll in the temple courts. Tradition, in itself, wasn't the problem. The problem He kept running into was specific: human traditions had been elevated to the level of divine command, and in some cases, those traditions were actively canceling out what God had actually said. In Mark 7:13, He named it plainly. The Pharisees were "making the word of God of no effect through your tradition which you have handed down." That's not a mild critique. That's a diagnosis of a very serious condition. And it didn't die with the Pharisees.

The Tradition Spectrum

Not all tradition is the same. That's the first thing to get clear, because the moment someone starts questioning religious habits, the conversation tends to collapse into two camps. One camp treats all tradition as suspect, as if anything older than last Sunday's sermon is probably man-made and therefore dangerous. The other camp treats all tradition as sacred, as if questioning any inherited practice is the same as questioning God Himself. Both of those positions miss the actual picture Scripture gives us.

Paul uses the word "tradition" in two very different ways, and both uses are in the Bible. In 2 Thessalonians 2:15, he tells believers to "hold to the traditions which you were taught, whether by word of mouth or by letter from us." That's a positive use. He's talking about the apostolic teaching, the gospel itself, the core of what was received from Christ and passed on faithfully. In 1 Corinthians 11:2, he commends the Corinthians for holding to the traditions he delivered to them. Tradition, in this sense, is the faithful transmission of what is true. It's how the gospel gets from one generation to the next without getting lost.

Then there's the other kind. Colossians 2:20-23 describes human regulations that "have an appearance of wisdom" but are "of no value against the indulgence of the flesh." They look spiritual. They feel serious. They might even produce a certain kind of religious pride. But they don't actually do what only the Spirit of God can do. They're human constructions wearing the clothes of divine command.

Think of it as a spectrum. On one end, you have apostolic tradition, the things directly rooted in Scripture and the teaching of Christ. The Lord's Supper. Baptism. The proclamation of the gospel. The gathered worship of believers around the Word. These aren't optional features of Christian life. They're commanded. They carry genuine authority because their authority comes from God, not from human preference or cultural habit.

On the other end, you have traditions that directly contradict or replace what Scripture says. These are the ones Jesus confronted most sharply. The Pharisees had developed a tradition called Corban, where a person could declare their money dedicated to God as a way of avoiding their responsibility to care for aging parents. The tradition looked religious. It used God's name. But it was being used to cancel out the clear command to honor your father and mother. That's not a neutral custom. That's a tradition functioning as a replacement for obedience.

In the middle sits a large and important category: neutral traditions. Practices that aren't commanded in Scripture, aren't forbidden in Scripture, and serve as helpful customs for ordering church life and personal devotion. The specific order of a worship service. Whether you kneel or stand to pray. Whether your church uses a liturgy or a more spontaneous format. Whether you observe the Christian calendar or not. Whether your pastor wears a robe or jeans. None of these things are prescribed in the New Testament in specific detail. They're human decisions made to serve the larger purpose of worshipping God together. There's nothing wrong with them. The danger comes when they drift from the middle of the spectrum toward one of the ends, specifically when they start being treated as if they carry the same authority as Scripture itself.

The Reformers had a memorable way of naming this distinction. They said that tradition, at its best, is "the living faith of dead people." The saints who came before us worshipped God, studied Scripture, developed practices and forms that helped them live faithfully, and passed those things on. That's a gift. We're richer for it. But when that living faith gets frozen into non-negotiable forms that can no longer be questioned, it becomes something else. It becomes, as the Reformers put it, "the dead faith of living people." The form survives. The life inside it doesn't. And a community that's practicing the dead faith of living people can look very busy, very religious, and very committed, while being almost entirely cut off from the actual movement of the Spirit.

Isaiah saw this pattern centuries before Jesus named it. In Isaiah 29:13, God said of His people: "Their fear toward Me is taught by the commandment of men." They were going through the motions of reverence. The outward forms were intact. But the reverence itself had been scripted by human instruction rather than produced by genuine encounter with God. Jesus quoted that exact verse when He confronted the Pharisees in Mark 7. The prophetic warning and the New Testament confrontation are pointing at the same thing across seven centuries: when human tradition teaches people how to feel about God rather than Scripture revealing who God actually is, the worship that results is hollow regardless of how sincere it looks.

The areas where traditions tend to accumulate most heavily in church life are worth naming specifically, because awareness is the first step toward honest evaluation. Worship service order is one of the most common. Most churches follow a fairly predictable sequence of events on Sunday morning, and that sequence is almost entirely a human decision. There's nothing wrong with having a consistent order. But when that order becomes so fixed that any variation feels like a violation, when the form has become more important than the function it was designed to serve, something has shifted. The same applies to the titles and qualifications of church leaders, the observance of religious holidays, the architecture and aesthetics of church spaces, the role of clergy versus the participation of ordinary believers. None of these categories are neutral in practice. All of them are areas where inherited custom can quietly take on the weight of divine command without anyone consciously deciding that's what happened.

The tradition audit is the practical tool for working through this. It's a set of five questions you can apply to any practice, personal or communal, to figure out where it sits on the spectrum and whether it's serving its intended purpose. Work through these questions honestly for any tradition you're examining. First: is this practice directly commanded in Scripture? Second: is it a helpful custom with no clear biblical basis either for or against it? Third: has this practice become so entrenched that questioning it feels like heresy, even to you? Fourth: does this practice produce the fruit of the Spirit in the people who observe it, or does it produce religious pride and boundary-marking? Fifth: would you, and would your community, be willing to lay this down if the Spirit clearly directed you to? The answers to those five questions will tell you almost everything you need to know about where a tradition sits and what it's actually doing in your life.

Sola Scriptura in Practice

The Reformation principle of sola Scriptura is one of the most misunderstood ideas in Protestant Christianity. People often hear it as a rejection of all tradition, as if the Reformers were saying that nothing matters except the Bible read in isolation from every other influence. That's not what it means. Sola Scriptura doesn't say that tradition has no value. It says that Scripture alone holds the final authority to judge, affirm, or reform every tradition. There's a significant difference between those two positions, and getting that difference right changes how you approach the whole question of inherited religious practice.

Think of it this way. A judge in a courtroom doesn't ignore the arguments made by lawyers on both sides. They listen to testimony, consider evidence, and weigh what's been presented. But at the end of the process, the judge makes a ruling based on the law, not based on which argument was more emotionally compelling or which lawyer had more years of experience. Sola Scriptura treats Scripture like that judge. Tradition gets to speak. History gets to inform. The wisdom of past generations gets to be heard. But Scripture makes the final call. And if what tradition says conflicts with what Scripture says, Scripture wins. Every time. Without apology.

The Bereans in Acts 17:11 are the New Testament model for this. When Paul arrived in Berea and began teaching, the text says the Bereans "received the word with all readiness, and searched the Scriptures daily to find out whether these things were so." They weren't being disrespectful to Paul. They were being faithful to the standard he himself had taught them. They didn't accept even apostolic teaching without checking it against Scripture. They were, in the best sense, testing the tradition being handed to them before they received it as authoritative.

That's the posture sola Scriptura is calling you to. Not cynicism toward everything inherited. Not the arrogance of assuming you understand the Bible better than everyone who came before you. But a genuine, disciplined willingness to hold every practice, every inherited form, every assumed-to-be-sacred custom up to the light of Scripture and ask honestly: does this hold up? Is this what God actually said? Or is this what my tradition says God said, which is a different thing entirely?

Galatians 1:13-14 gives us Paul's own testimony about this process. He describes his former life as someone who was "extremely zealous for the traditions of his fathers." He wasn't a casual observer of Jewish religious custom. He was one of its most committed practitioners. He'd studied under the best teachers. He'd advanced beyond his peers in his dedication to the inherited forms. And then he encountered the risen Christ, and everything he'd been so zealously protecting had to be re-evaluated. Not thrown out wholesale. But honestly weighed against the reality of who Jesus is. And what didn't hold up, he let go, even though it had been central to his identity for his entire life. That's not a small thing to do. Paul knew it wasn't small. But he also knew that what he'd found in Christ was worth more than what he was releasing.

The practical work of sola Scriptura looks like this. You take a specific practice, something you do regularly as part of your faith life, and you ask a direct question: where does this come from? If the answer is "the Bible says so," your next step is to find the actual passage. Not a passage that sort of relates to it, or a passage that could be interpreted to support it if you read it in a particular way. The actual passage where God commands or clearly commends this practice. If you find it, great. The practice has a foundation. If you can't find it, that doesn't automatically mean the practice is wrong. It means it's somewhere in the middle of the spectrum, a human custom rather than a divine command. And that changes how you should hold it. You hold it with an open hand rather than a closed fist. You benefit from it when it helps you. You're free to lay it down when it stops helping or when it starts getting in the way of something God is actually asking for.

The areas where this kind of examination tends to produce the most significant results are the ones that feel the most sacred. Not the obviously optional things, but the things that have acquired an almost unquestionable status in your spiritual life. The specific way you structure your personal devotions. The particular worship style you believe is most honoring to God. The theological framework you've inherited about end times, church government, or spiritual gifts. The denominational distinctives you've absorbed as simply "what the Bible teaches" without ever tracing them back to see whether that's actually true. These are the places where honest Berean examination is most needed and most resisted.

Take someone like a hypothetical 38-year-old named Claire, who grew up in a liturgical church tradition. Every Sunday of her childhood followed the same structure: the call to worship, the confession, the Gloria, the readings, the sermon, the Eucharist, the benediction. She loves it. It shaped her. It gave her a deep sense of the weight and holiness of approaching God. When she married and moved to a new city, she started attending her husband's non-liturgical church, and the informality felt almost irreverent to her. The lack of structure seemed to her like a lack of seriousness. She found herself judging the worship as shallow, not because she'd examined the biblical case for liturgy versus non-liturgy, but because what was unfamiliar felt wrong. The tradition she'd inherited had quietly become the standard by which she measured everything else. That's not sola Scriptura. That's traditionalism. And it was costing her the ability to receive genuine worship from a community that was simply ordering their encounter with God differently than she was used to.

The answer for Claire isn't to abandon her liturgical tradition. The answer is to hold it the way it was meant to be held: as a form that serves the encounter with God rather than a form that defines what that encounter must look like. When she can do that, she gains something. She keeps the richness of her inherited practice and gains the freedom to recognize God's presence in forms that look different from the ones she grew up with. That's what sola Scriptura actually produces in a person who applies it honestly. Not the stripping away of everything familiar. The recovery of the freedom to let Scripture, rather than inherited preference, be the final word on what matters most.

The question that cuts to the heart of this for most believers is the one that's hardest to sit with honestly: has any practice in your spiritual life become so entrenched that questioning it feels like questioning God? If the answer is yes, that's not a sign of deep faith. That's a sign that a human tradition has been elevated to the level of divine command. And that's exactly the condition Jesus addressed in Mark 7. The discomfort you feel when someone questions a deeply held practice is worth paying attention to. It's telling you something about where your security is actually located. If it's located in the practice rather than in the God the practice is supposed to point to, the practice has become an obstacle rather than a help.

The Emotional Weight of Heritage

None of this is as clean as it sounds on paper. That needs to be said directly, because a chapter that talks about tradition audits and sola Scriptura without acknowledging the emotional weight of what it's asking can feel cold and clinical in a way that isn't honest about the actual human experience of questioning inherited faith.

Traditions aren't just theological positions. They're memories. They're the smell of a particular church building on Sunday morning. They're the hymn your mother sang while she cooked dinner. They're the way your father prayed before meals, the specific words he used, the posture he took, the reverence in his voice. They're the Christmas Eve service you've attended every year of your life. They're the theological framework your pastor taught you when you were seventeen and first taking your faith seriously. These things aren't just ideas. They're woven into your identity, your family bonds, your sense of who you are and where you belong.

When someone questions a tradition that's tied to all of that, it doesn't feel like a theological discussion. It feels like an attack on something you love. And the instinct to defend it isn't just intellectual stubbornness. It's something much more human than that. It's the protection of something that matters to you at a level that goes deeper than argument.

That's worth honoring. Not by refusing to examine the tradition, but by being honest about the cost of examining it. Paul knew this cost personally. When he described his former zeal for the traditions of his fathers in Galatians 1, he wasn't describing something he'd held lightly. He'd built his entire identity around those traditions. His education, his social standing, his sense of righteousness, his belonging to a community he loved, all of it was wrapped up in what he was being called to re-evaluate in light of Christ. Letting go of what didn't hold up wasn't a casual decision. It was costly. And he never pretended otherwise.

The pastoral wisdom here is this: you can hold the tension between honoring your heritage and being honest about its limitations. These aren't mutually exclusive. You can be grateful for what a tradition gave you while being honest about where it has gone beyond what Scripture actually supports. You can love the community that shaped you while being willing to ask hard questions about the practices that community treats as non-negotiable. You can honor your parents' faith while recognizing that their faith, like yours, is a work in progress, not a finished product to be preserved unchanged.

The key is to separate the tradition from the people who carried it to you. Your grandmother's faith was real. Her love for God was genuine. The practices she passed on to you came from a sincere heart. None of that is in question. What's in question is whether every specific form her faith took was directly commanded by God or whether some of it was the particular shape her culture and generation gave to a genuine encounter with God. You can honor her faith while asking that question honestly. In fact, if her faith was as genuine as you believe it was, she'd probably want you to.

There's also a specific kind of courage required when the tradition being questioned is one that your current community holds sacred. It's one thing to privately re-evaluate a practice. It's another thing to raise questions in a community where those questions aren't welcome. The social cost of being the person who asks "but where does the Bible actually say that?" in a room full of people who've never thought to ask it can be significant. You might be seen as troublesome. You might lose standing. You might find that the community's tolerance for honest examination is narrower than you thought. That's a real cost, and it's worth naming honestly.

But consider what's at stake on the other side of that cost. A faith that can't be examined is a faith that can't grow. A community that can't ask hard questions about its own practices is a community that will eventually calcify around the practices rather than around Christ. The willingness to ask honest questions, with humility and genuine love for the community, is itself an act of faithfulness. It's not disloyalty. It's the Berean spirit applied to the community you actually belong to.

The way to hold this tension well is to be clear about your motivation. There's a difference between questioning tradition out of pride, out of a desire to be contrarian, out of a need to feel more spiritually sophisticated than the people around you, and questioning tradition out of a genuine desire to ensure that your faith and your community's faith is actually rooted in what God said rather than in what humans assumed He said. The first motivation produces division. The second produces reformation. And the difference is usually visible in how you go about it. Do you raise questions with love for the community, with genuine humility about your own blind spots, with a willingness to be wrong? Or do you raise them with contempt, with the posture of someone who's already decided they've figured out what everyone else has missed? The posture matters as much as the question.

Prioritizing Christ above heritage doesn't mean treating heritage as worthless. It means treating Christ as primary. When those two things come into conflict, and sometimes they will, Christ wins. Not heritage. Not family expectation. Not community belonging. Not the fear of what people will think if you start asking questions. Christ. That's the simplicity of devotion Paul describes in 2 Corinthians 11:3, the sincere and pure devotion to Christ that can get complicated and cluttered by all the things that accumulate around it over time. Recovering that simplicity isn't about becoming a theological minimalist. It's about making sure that everything you carry is actually serving the center rather than obscuring it.

Your Tradition Audit: Specific Steps

Everything in this chapter has been building toward a practical question: what are you actually going to do with this? Insight without action stays abstract. The tradition audit isn't a concept to admire. It's a tool to use. The following steps will walk you through applying it specifically to your own life over the next two weeks.

Step one: List three specific traditions you currently practice and research their biblical basis. Pick three practices that are regular parts of your faith life. They can be personal devotional habits or things your church does corporately. For each one, write down where you think it comes from. Then do the actual research. Open your Bible and look for the passage that commands or clearly commends this practice. Use a concordance if you need to. If you find a clear biblical basis, write it down beside the practice. If you find a passage that's been interpreted to support it but doesn't directly command it, note that distinction. If you can't find a biblical basis at all, note that too. You're not trying to condemn the practice. You're trying to know what you're actually holding and why. This exercise takes about an hour per tradition if you do it honestly. Do all three before moving to the next step.

Step two: Apply all five audit questions to each tradition you researched. Go back to the five questions from the tradition spectrum section. Is it commanded in Scripture? Is it a helpful neutral custom? Has it become so entrenched that questioning it feels like heresy? Does it produce the fruit of the Spirit or religious pride? Would you be willing to lay it down if the Spirit directed you to? Write your honest answers to each question for each tradition. Don't rush this. The answers to question three and question four are especially important. If a practice has become so sacred that you can't imagine questioning it, and if the primary fruit it produces in you is a sense of being right or being more serious about God than others, those are significant warning signs. Write them down rather than explaining them away.

Step three: Identify one tradition that needs to be held more loosely, and make one specific change in how you hold it this

week. Based on your audit, pick the tradition that most clearly sits in the middle of the spectrum, a helpful custom that you've been treating as a divine command. The change you make doesn't have to be dramatic. It might be as simple as trying a different format for your personal prayer time for one week to see whether the format or the content is what actually matters. It might be attending a worship service in a different style than you're used to, specifically to practice recognizing God's presence in an unfamiliar form. It might be having one honest conversation with a trusted friend about a practice your community holds sacred, asking together where it actually comes from. The goal of this step is to loosen your grip on the form enough to check whether what you're actually holding onto is the form or the God the form is supposed to serve. Write down what you're going to do and when you're going to do it before you close this chapter.

Step four: Pray specifically about one tradition tied to family or community heritage that you've never honestly examined. This is the emotionally hardest step, which is why it comes last. Think of one practice that's connected to people you love, to memories that matter, to a community that's shaped you. Something you've never questioned not because you've examined it and found it solid, but because questioning it has always felt like a betrayal of something precious. Bring that practice to God in prayer, not with the goal of deciding to abandon it, but with the honest question: "God, is this serving you, or has it become something I'm protecting for reasons that aren't about you?" Sit with that question for at least ten minutes in silence. Write down whatever surfaces. You're not obligated to act on what you hear immediately. But you are obligated to hear it honestly rather than deflecting it before it has a chance to reach you.

The goal of all of this is the same goal that runs through this entire book. A faith that's actually alive rather than just familiar. A devotion to Christ that's simple enough to be real, and honest enough to let Scripture have the final word over every inherited assumption. That kind of faith doesn't strip away everything that came before. It holds what's genuinely apostolic with both hands and holds what's merely human with an open palm, grateful for what it offered and free to release it when it stops serving the One it was always supposed to point toward.

The traditions we carry aren't the problem. The problem is when we stop being able to tell the difference between the ones God gave us and the ones we gave ourselves. That distinction is worth every bit of the honest, humble, sometimes uncomfortable work it takes to find it.

6

**THE ALLURE OF SPECULATIVE
ESCHATOLOGY**

The Allure of Speculative Eschatology

There's a particular kind of Christian bookstore shelf that tells you a lot about where the church's imagination has been living for the past several decades. Charts. Timelines. Color-coded diagrams mapping out the sequence of end-times events with the kind of confidence you'd expect from someone who'd just returned from the future. Books with titles that feel urgent, almost breathless, as if the author barely had time to write them before everything fell apart. And underneath all of it, a quiet but persistent message: if you don't understand the timeline, you're missing something critical.

Millions of sincere Christians have absorbed that message. And it's worth asking honestly what it's produced in them.

This chapter isn't an attack on any particular theological tradition. People who hold premillennial or dispensational views aren't being dismissed here. Many of them are serious, Scripture-loving believers who've thought carefully about these texts. The concern isn't the eschatological system itself. The concern is what happens to any system when it shifts from "live faithfully because Jesus is coming" to "figure out the timeline because Jesus is coming." That shift, subtle as it sounds, changes everything. It changes what you read. It changes what you fear. It changes what you talk about at the dinner table and what keeps you awake at three in the morning. And in too many cases, it changes a faith that was supposed to produce holiness and hope into something that produces anxiety and paralysis instead.

From Charts to Character

The modern obsession with end-times timelines didn't appear out of nowhere. It has a traceable history, and understanding that history helps you see it more clearly for what it is.

In the nineteenth century, a theologian named John Nelson Darby developed a detailed system for interpreting biblical prophecy called dispensationalism. He divided history into distinct eras or "dispensations," each with its own set of divine arrangements, and he mapped out a specific sequence of end-times events including a rapture, a seven-year tribulation, and a literal thousand-year reign of Christ on earth. His ideas were compelling and detailed, and they spread rapidly through the Scofield Reference Bible, which was published in 1909 and became one of the most widely used study Bibles in American Protestant history. The Scofield Bible had Darby's dispensational framework built directly into its footnotes, sitting right alongside the biblical text. For generations of readers, the framework and the text felt like one thing, not two. The interpretive system was so embedded in how the Bible was presented that millions of people absorbed it as simply "what the Bible says" without ever realizing they were reading a particular theological lens alongside Scripture itself.

Then came Hal Lindsey.

In 1970, Lindsey published "The Late Great Planet Earth," and it became one of the best-selling non-fiction books of the entire decade.

He took Darby's framework and applied it directly to current events, mapping Cold War geopolitics onto biblical prophecy with a confidence that felt electrifying. The Soviet Union was Gog and Magog. The European Common Market was the revived Roman Empire. Israel's return to the land in 1948 was the "fig tree" generation Jesus spoke of in Matthew 24, which Lindsey argued meant the rapture would happen within forty years. The book sold millions of copies. It shaped a generation's imagination about what the future held and what faithful Christians should be paying attention to.

The "Left Behind" series, beginning in 1995, took that imagination and turned it into narrative. Sixteen novels. Eighty million copies sold. A fictional account of the rapture and its aftermath that was so vivid, so specific, and so emotionally compelling that for many readers it became the mental picture they carried when they thought about end-times events. Not a theological framework. A story. With characters they knew and a sequence of events they could follow. The power of that kind of narrative to shape belief is enormous, and it's worth being honest about how much of what many Christians "know" about the end times comes from those novels rather than from careful study of the biblical text itself.

The point isn't that every idea in these works is wrong. The point is that together they created something the New Testament never intended: a consumer culture around eschatology. A marketplace of fear, speculation, and sensationalism with its own publishing industry, its own celebrity teachers, its own conferences and DVDs and YouTube channels, all of it generating revenue from the anxiety of people who've been convinced that understanding the timeline is urgent, that identifying the Antichrist is critical, that figuring out where current events fit on the prophetic calendar is something a serious Christian simply must do.

That's a significant thing to name. Because what it means is that for many believers, eschatology stopped being a call to live differently and became a hobby. An intellectual puzzle. A framework for interpreting the news. And the more time and emotional energy a person pours into that puzzle, the less time and energy they have for the things the New Testament actually says the return of Christ should produce in a person's life.

Think about what this looks like in practice. Consider a hypothetical person, a 42-year-old named David, who grew up in a church deeply shaped by dispensational teaching. He's a thoughtful man. He loves God. He reads his Bible. But for the past several years, a significant portion of his spiritual energy has gone toward watching prophecy teachers on YouTube, tracking news headlines for signs of the times, and debating the sequence of end-times events with friends in his small group. He feels like this is being a faithful watchman. He feels like he's paying attention to what matters. But when you look at the actual fruit of all this focus, something concerning surfaces. He's more anxious than he was five years ago, not less. He's more suspicious of institutions, more prone to seeing conspiracy, more divided from fellow believers who hold different eschatological views. His prayer life is mostly petition for God to protect him from what's coming rather than intercession for the people around him. His evangelism has nearly stopped because in his mind, the world is so close to judgment that long-term investment in relationships feels almost pointless. He's watching. But he's not ready. And he doesn't realize the difference.

That's what fear-based eschatology produces when it runs its full course. Not faithfulness. Not holiness. A posture of anxious surveillance that mistakes information-gathering for spiritual readiness.

Jesus was direct about this. In Mark 13:32-37, He said plainly that no one knows the day or hour of His return. Not the angels. Not even the Son in His earthly ministry. Only the Father. And His instruction following that statement wasn't "therefore study harder so you can narrow it down." It was "watch and be ready." Two different things entirely. Watching in the sense Jesus meant isn't scanning headlines for prophetic fulfillment. It's the watchfulness of a servant who stays faithful to their master's instructions regardless of when the master returns. The servant who's watching in the right sense isn't spending their time trying to calculate the master's arrival time. They're making sure that whenever the master walks through the door, the work is done and done well.

The parable of the wise and foolish virgins in Matthew 25:1-13 makes this even clearer. All ten virgins knew the bridegroom was coming. All ten were waiting for him. The difference between the wise and foolish wasn't knowledge of the timeline. It was preparedness. The wise ones had oil. The foolish ones didn't. And when the bridegroom came at midnight, the foolish ones discovered that no amount of last-minute scrambling could substitute for the preparation they'd neglected. Jesus ends the parable with a statement that cuts straight to the heart of the matter: "You do not know the day or the hour." That's not a problem to be solved by more research. It's a condition that makes present faithfulness the only appropriate response.

The parable of the talents, which immediately follows in Matthew 25:14-30, reinforces the same point from a different angle. The master goes away. He doesn't tell the servants when he's coming back. And the servants who are commended aren't the ones who spent their time trying to figure out his return schedule. They're the ones who took what they were given and put it to work. The servant who buried his talent, who essentially did nothing while waiting for the master to return, is the one who faces judgment. Inactivity dressed as caution isn't faithfulness. It's exactly the kind of paralysis that fear-based eschatology produces in people who've convinced themselves that the most important thing they can do is watch and wait.

There's also a practical problem with certain strands of speculative eschatology that doesn't get talked about enough. When the world is seen as irredeemably lost, as destined only for destruction with no redemptive future worth investing in, it produces a "why bother?" attitude toward things that Scripture clearly calls believers to care about. Justice for the vulnerable. Care for creation. Long-term investment in communities and relationships and institutions. If the whole thing is burning down anyway, the logic goes, why plant trees? Why work for structural change? Why build anything meant to last? That logic feels spiritual but it's actually a form of irresponsibility dressed in prophetic language. A balanced biblical eschatology holds both realities simultaneously: yes, Christ is returning and history is moving toward a definite end, and yes, believers are called to be salt and light in the present age, which means their actions in the world right now actually matter. Both are true. Collapsing one into the other produces a distorted faith.

Deuteronomy 29:29 draws a line that's worth respecting. "The secret things belong to the Lord our God, but those things which are revealed belong to us and to our children forever, that we may do all the words of this law." God has deliberately kept certain things hidden. The exact timing of Christ's return is one of them. He hasn't hidden it because He forgot to tell us or because we haven't studied hard enough. He's hidden it because knowing it would actually undermine the posture of readiness He's looking for. A servant who knows exactly when the master is coming doesn't need faithfulness. They just need a calendar. The uncertainty is the point. It's what makes present faithfulness the only rational response to the reality of Christ's return.

The two eschatological postures are worth holding side by side very clearly. The first asks, "Is this the Antichrist? Is that the mark? Where does this news event fit on the prophetic calendar?" The second asks, "Lord, find me faithful whenever you return." The first produces fear, division, and a consuming preoccupation with information. The second produces holiness, love, and active mission. The first treats the return of Christ as a puzzle to be solved. The second treats it as a reality to be ready for. These aren't equally valid approaches. One of them is what the New Testament consistently models. The other is what the Christian publishing industry has spent decades selling.

The Purpose of Prophecy

The most important corrective to speculative eschatology isn't a better eschatological system. It's a recovered understanding of what biblical prophecy is actually for.

Peter addresses this directly in 2 Peter 1:19-21. He describes the prophetic word as "a lamp shining in a dark place until the day dawns and the morning star rises in your hearts." Read that image carefully. A lamp shining in a dark place. What does a lamp do? It illuminates the space you're currently standing in. It shows you where to put your foot next. It reveals what's immediately around you so you can move through the darkness without falling. A lamp isn't a telescope. It doesn't show you what's happening on the other side of the mountain. It shows you what's right in front of you, right now, so you can walk faithfully through the present moment.

That's what Peter says prophecy is. A lamp for the present. Not a crystal ball for the future.

The prophets of the Old Testament understood this. When Isaiah spoke about the coming servant of the Lord, the primary purpose wasn't to give his readers a detailed preview of events seven hundred years away. The primary purpose was to call his readers to faithfulness in the present. To show them who God is and what He's doing, so they could align their lives with His purposes right now. The future element was real. But it served the present call. The vision of what God would do was meant to shape how His people lived in the meantime.

The apostles used eschatology exactly this way. Look at how Paul handles it in 1 Thessalonians 5:1-11. He talks about the day of the Lord coming like a thief in the night. He describes the sudden destruction that will come on those who are unprepared. And then, immediately, his application is entirely ethical. "Therefore let us not sleep, as others do, but let us watch and be sober." Not "therefore let us study the signs more carefully." Not "therefore let us identify who the man of lawlessness might be." Watch and be sober. Live in a way that's consistent with being children of the light. Encourage one another. Build each other up. The eschatological reality lands directly on how to live today. That's how Paul always uses it.

Peter does the same thing in 2 Peter 3:11-14. He describes the coming dissolution of everything, the heavens and earth passing away with a great noise, the elements melting with fervent heat. And his application is a question that cuts to the heart of the matter: "Since all these things will be dissolved, what manner of persons ought you to be in holy conduct and godliness?" The future reality of Christ's return and the dissolution of the present order is meant to produce a specific kind of present life. Holy conduct. Godliness. Diligence to be found by Him in peace, without spot and blameless. The future doesn't produce paralysis. It produces urgency about character.

Titus 2:12-13 captures this in a single breath. The grace of God teaches us to "deny ungodliness and worldly lusts" and to "live soberly, righteously, and godly in the present age, looking for the blessed hope and glorious appearing of our great God and Savior Jesus Christ." Looking for the blessed hope. That's the eschatological posture Paul commends. Not anxious surveillance of current events. Not speculative calculation of timelines. Looking. With hope. And that looking produces a specific kind of present life: sober, righteous, godly. The return of Christ is the horizon that gives present faithfulness its meaning and its urgency.

First John 3:2-3 is perhaps the clearest statement of all. "Beloved, now we are children of God; and it has not yet been revealed what we shall be, but we know that when He is revealed, we shall be like Him, for we shall see Him as He is. And everyone who has this hope in Him purifies himself, just as He is pure." Read that carefully. The hope of seeing Christ as He is produces purification. Not speculation. Not anxiety. Purification. The person who genuinely hopes in Christ's return becomes more like Christ in the present. That's the fruit of a healthy eschatology. Not a detailed timeline. A purified life.

This is the pattern across the entire New Testament. Every time Jesus or the apostles teach about the future, the application lands on the present. It lands on how you treat people. On whether you're faithful with what you've been given. On whether you're living with the kind of integrity that would make you unashamed when Christ appears. The future is always in service of the present call. When that relationship gets inverted, when the present gets subordinated to speculative future-mapping, something has gone wrong with the way prophecy is being used.

Revelation 1:1-3 is worth noting here. The book that has generated more eschatological speculation than perhaps any other text in history opens with a clear statement of its purpose. It was given "to show His servants things which must shortly take place." And the text immediately pronounces a blessing on "he who reads and those who hear the words of this prophecy, and keep those things which are written in it." Keep those things. The blessing isn't on those who decode the timeline. It's on those who keep what's written. The purpose of Revelation, stated in its own opening verses, is pastoral and practical. It was written to churches under pressure, to give them the perspective they needed to stay faithful in the middle of real suffering and real persecution. It was a lamp for their present darkness. Not a puzzle for curious future readers to solve.

The specific way the apostles used eschatological teaching is worth cataloging, because the pattern is so consistent that it becomes impossible to miss once you see it. In 1 Corinthians 15:58, after his extended argument for the resurrection, Paul lands here: "Therefore, my beloved brethren, be steadfast, immovable, always abounding in the work of the Lord, knowing that your labor is not in vain in the Lord." The resurrection hope produces steadfastness and active labor in the present. In 1 John 3:3, as already noted, hope produces purification. In Titus 2:12-13, the blessed hope produces present godliness. In 1 Thessalonians 5, the day of the Lord coming like a thief produces sobriety, watchfulness, and mutual encouragement. The application is always ethical. Always missional. Always about how to live right now. That's not a coincidence. That's the consistent apostolic model for how eschatological truth is supposed to function in a believer's life.

When prophecy becomes an intellectual puzzle rather than a call to obedience, something has gone wrong. That's not a harsh judgment. It's an observation about function. A lamp that's being studied as an artifact rather than used for illumination isn't doing what it was made to do. Biblical prophecy was given to light the path of present faithfulness. When it gets turned into an object of speculation, it stops illuminating the path and starts becoming a distraction from it.

The contrast between the two postures is stark when you lay them side by side. Fear-based eschatology produces anxiety about the future, preoccupation with identifying signs and actors, division among believers over interpretive details, and a kind of cultural disengagement that masquerades as spiritual discernment. Hope-based eschatology produces peace about the future, urgency about present faithfulness, unity around the shared hope of Christ's return, and active engagement with the world as salt and light. The first posture is turned inward and backward, trying to decode what's already happened and predict what's next. The second posture is turned outward and forward, asking what faithful presence looks like in the time that's been given.

The question that matters isn't "have I correctly identified the Antichrist?" The question is "would I be found faithful if Christ returned today?" Those are very different questions. They produce very different lives. And only one of them is the question the New Testament actually asks you to be able to answer.

Recap and What to Do Now

The core of what this chapter has been building toward is simple enough to state in one sentence: hope-driven eschatology produces holiness, while fear-based systems produce paralysis. That's not just a theological observation. It's a diagnostic tool. You can look at the fruit of how you've been engaging with end-times teaching and know immediately which kind of eschatology has been shaping you. If the primary emotions are anxiety, suspicion, and a consuming need to track current events against prophetic charts, the teaching has been fear-based regardless of what it claimed to be. If the primary fruit is a deepened commitment to personal holiness, a greater urgency about the people around you who don't know Christ, and a settled peace that comes from knowing the story ends with Jesus winning, the posture is healthy.

The following steps are specific. They're designed to move you from wherever you are right now toward the posture the New Testament consistently models. Work through them in order.

First: Stop consuming sensationalist prophecy media for thirty days, completely and specifically. This isn't a vague suggestion to "be careful about what you watch." It's a concrete action. Identify the specific sources that have been feeding an anxious, speculative engagement with end-times teaching. The YouTube channels. The podcasts. The prophecy news websites. The social media accounts that post about signs of the times. Stop all of them for thirty days. Not forever. Thirty days. The goal is to create enough silence around this topic that you can hear what your actual spiritual condition sounds like without the constant noise of speculation. When you stop, pay attention to what surfaces. If stopping feels almost impossible, if the pull to check back in is strong and uncomfortable, that's important information about how much of your spiritual attention this content has been consuming.

Second: Read 1 John slowly, one chapter per day for five days, looking specifically for what it says hope produces. Don't read it looking for eschatological content. Read it looking for the connection between future hope and present life. Write down every verse where John connects what we know about Christ's return or our future in Him to how we should live right now. Pay special attention to 1 John 3:2-3. Write out that passage by hand and put it somewhere visible. The practice of reading it daily for one week does something to your imagination about the future that no amount of prophetic chart-study can do. It replaces the image of an anxious watcher scanning the horizon for threats with the image of a child of God who is being purified by the hope of seeing their Father face to face.

Third: Write out a specific answer to this question: what would change in your daily life if your primary focus about the future shifted from "figuring it out" to "being ready"? Don't answer this in your head. Write it down. Be specific. Would you pray differently? Would you invest more in the people immediately around you? Would you stop some of the anxious news consumption that's been eating your time and attention? Would you start something you've been putting off because the world feels too unstable? Write at least five specific things that would change. Then pick one of them and start it this week. Not next month. This week. The shift from speculative watching to faithful readiness isn't primarily a theological adjustment. It's a practical one. It shows up in how you spend Tuesday afternoon, not just in what you believe about the tribulation.

Fourth: Find one person in your life who doesn't know Christ and invest specifically in that relationship this month. This is the missional application of everything in this chapter. The return of Christ is the most urgent reason to care about the people around you who aren't ready for it. Not because you need to frighten them with end-times scenarios, but because you genuinely love them and you know that what's coming is real. Identify one person. Not a category of people. One specific person. Write their name down. Then make one concrete plan to spend meaningful time with them this month. A meal. A conversation. A regular point of contact that's about genuine relationship rather than a program. This is what "abounding in the work of the Lord" looks like in practice. It's not decoding prophecy. It's loving the person in front of you with the urgency that comes from knowing time is real and Christ is coming.

The return of Christ is one of the most glorious promises in all of Scripture. It's meant to be a source of deep, settled, active hope. The kind of hope that purifies you. The kind that makes you more loving, more generous, more faithful, more present to the people around you. When that hope gets twisted into a system of fear and speculation, it doesn't just fail to produce those things. It actively works against them. Recovering the biblical posture toward Christ's return isn't a small adjustment. It's a reorientation of the entire emotional and spiritual register with which you engage the future. And that reorientation, lived out in the ordinary details of daily faithfulness, is exactly what it looks like to be a stranger in a culture of compromise. The world is anxious about the future. God's people are meant to be at peace, not because they've figured out the timeline, but because they know the One who holds it.

7

THE GOSPEL VERSUS FANATICISM

There's a kind of spiritual intensity that looks like devotion from the outside but feels like something else entirely when you're standing next to it. It talks about God constantly. It shares urgent warnings. It's always tracking the latest development, the newest threat, the most recent sign. It has a certainty that doesn't leave room for questions. And somehow, despite all that religious activity, the people around it don't feel loved. They feel managed, pressured, or judged. They feel like they're either insiders who get it or outsiders who don't.

That's fanaticism. And it's not the same thing as genuine faith, no matter how much biblical language it uses.

Chapter 6 looked at the content of speculative eschatology, the charts and timelines and anxious future-mapping that pulls believers away from present faithfulness. This chapter moves from content to character. Because the real problem with fanaticism isn't just what it teaches. It's what it produces in the people who follow it. And Jesus gave us a very clear tool for evaluating exactly that.

He said you'll know a tree by its fruit.

That's not a complicated test. It doesn't require a theology degree. It doesn't require insider knowledge of a particular movement's history or doctrinal nuances. It requires paying attention to what a teaching actually produces in the lives of the people who receive it. Does it make them more loving? More patient? More gentle with people who disagree? More rooted in Scripture, prayer, and the ordinary life of the local church? Or does it make them more anxious, more suspicious, more certain of their own rightness, and more contemptuous of anyone who hasn't seen what they've seen? The fruit answers the question. Every time.

The Fruit of the Spirit Diagnostic

Galatians 5 gives us two lists, and the contrast between them is worth sitting with carefully. The works of the flesh include strife, contentions, heresies, and envy. The fruit of the Spirit includes love, joy, peace, patience, kindness, goodness, faithfulness, gentleness, and self-control. Paul isn't describing two different theological systems. He's describing two different kinds of lives, two different sets of outcomes that flow from two different sources. And the test he's offering is remarkably practical. You don't need to analyze the doctrine. You look at the life. You look at the relationships. You look at what grows.

Fanaticism has a recognizable profile when you know what to look for.

It carries a sense of urgency that's completely disconnected from love. Everything is urgent. Every headline is a sign. Every disagreement is a spiritual battle. Every person who doesn't share the same level of alarm is either asleep or compromised. The urgency feels righteous from the inside, like a watchman on the wall doing what needs to be done. But it produces a kind of relentlessness that exhausts the people around it and crowds out the slower, quieter work of actually loving people well.

It holds a certainty that refuses correction. Not the kind of certainty that comes from years of humble study and tested faith. A brittle certainty that treats any pushback as spiritual attack. When someone raises a question, the fanatic doesn't engage the question. They question the questioner's motives, their spiritual discernment, their willingness to see what's really going on. This kind of certainty isn't confidence in God. It's confidence in one's own interpretation, which is a very different thing and a much more fragile one.

It fixates on enemies and threats. There's always a villain. A system. A group. A conspiracy. The narrative requires an enemy, and an enormous amount of mental and spiritual energy goes into tracking that enemy, exposing it, warning others about it. What gets crowded out is attention to the people immediately around you, the neighbor who needs help, the coworker going through a divorce, the family member who's quietly falling apart. Fanaticism is always looking past the person in front of it toward the threat on the horizon.

It produces contempt for those who disagree. Not just disagreement. Contempt. The person who doesn't see what the fanatic sees isn't just wrong. They're naive, compromised, spiritually blind, or part of the problem. That contempt is one of the clearest signs that something has gone wrong, because contempt and love cannot occupy the same heart at the same time. First Corinthians 13:1-3 is unambiguous about this: you can speak with the tongues of angels, you can have all knowledge, you can even give your body to be burned, and if you don't have love, you have nothing. Not less than you could have. Nothing.

And fanaticism neglects the ordinary means of grace. This is one of the most telling signs of all. When a person is deep in fanatical thinking, their Bible reading becomes almost entirely about finding confirmation for what they already believe. Their prayer life shrinks to petition for protection from the threats they're tracking. They stop sitting under consistent pastoral teaching. They pull away from local church community, because the local church feels too slow, too uninformed, too unwilling to take seriously what they're seeing. The spectacular claims and secret knowledge they're consuming online become the real spiritual diet, and the ordinary bread of Scripture, prayer, fellowship, communion, and service starts to feel insufficient by comparison.

Gospel maturity looks nothing like this. And the contrast isn't subtle.

Love, joy, peace, patience, kindness, goodness, faithfulness, gentleness, self-control. Not one of those nine qualities is sensational. Not one of them will get you a large online following. Not one of them generates the kind of urgent engagement that social media rewards. But every single one of them is a testimony to the presence of the Holy Spirit in a person's life, and together they describe exactly the kind of person that the world around them can't quite explain. A person who is genuinely patient with difficult people. Who carries real peace in genuinely uncertain times. Who treats opponents with kindness rather than contempt. Who stays gentle when they could be harsh. That person is a stranger in a culture of compromise in the truest sense, not because they're louder than everyone else, but because they're different in ways that actually cost something.

It's important to say something clearly here, because this chapter could be misread as an argument against spiritual passion or prophetic urgency. It isn't. The church needs people who feel things deeply, who carry genuine concern for truth, who are willing to say hard things when hard things need to be said. The issue isn't passion. The issue is what happens to passion when it gets disconnected from love, from accountability, and from the fruit of the Spirit. Fiery devotion that is also gentle, humble, and kind is one of the most powerful forces on earth. Fiery devotion that has lost its gentleness and its humility is just fire. And fire without those things burns the people it was supposed to warm.

Proverbs 19:2 puts it plainly: "Desire without knowledge is not good, and whoever makes haste with his feet misses his way." Urgency alone doesn't make something true or right. Speed doesn't equal faithfulness. The person running fastest isn't necessarily running in the right direction. And the person who's most certain isn't necessarily the person who's most correct. These are things fanaticism forgets, and the forgetting is always costly.

First John 4:1-6 tells believers to test the spirits, because not every spirit is from God. The test John offers is twofold: does it confess Christ, and does it produce love? Those are the two non-negotiables. Not: does it have a compelling explanation for current events? Not: does it have insider knowledge that other teachers don't? Does it confess Christ? Does it produce love? If the answer to either of those questions is no, or even unclear, that's the answer you need. You don't need to investigate further. The test has already returned its result.

Think about someone like a hypothetical 39-year-old woman named Rachel, a sincere believer who started watching online prophecy teachers during a difficult season in her life. She was anxious, isolated, and genuinely searching for answers. The content she found felt urgent and spiritually serious. It gave her a sense of purpose and a feeling of being part of something important. But over the next two years, her closest relationships quietly deteriorated. She grew impatient with her husband, who didn't share her level of concern about what she was seeing. She pulled back from her small group because the conversations felt too shallow. She stopped serving in her church's children's ministry because she was spending those hours watching more content instead. She was consuming more spiritual material than ever in her life and becoming less loving, less present, and less rooted than she'd ever been. The fruit told the story her theology couldn't see. The tree she was eating from wasn't producing what the Spirit produces. And that's the test. Not the label on the bottle. What's actually in it.

Matthew 7:15-20 is worth quoting in full in your mind every time you encounter a new teaching or movement that's competing for your attention. "Beware of false prophets, who come to you in sheep's clothing, but inwardly they are ravenous wolves. You will know them by their fruits." Not by their credentials. Not by how many followers they have. Not by how detailed their prophetic knowledge seems to be. By their fruits. That's the test Jesus gave. It's the only one you need.

The Digital Echo Chamber

The mechanics of how fanaticism spreads have changed dramatically in the past fifteen years. What used to require a fringe church, a charismatic leader, and a physical gathering can now happen entirely through a phone screen, in the privacy of someone's bedroom, with no pastor, no accountability, and no community to push back on what's being consumed. This is one of the most significant spiritual challenges of the current moment, and the church hasn't fully reckoned with it yet.

Social media algorithms don't care about truth. They care about engagement. And the content that generates the most engagement, the most clicks, the most shares, the most time-on-platform, is almost never the content that's most accurate, most balanced, or most spiritually healthy. It's the content that triggers the strongest emotional response. Fear triggers engagement. Outrage triggers engagement. The promise of secret knowledge that explains what's really going on triggers engagement. The algorithm doesn't know the difference between a genuine prophetic warning and sensationalist religious conspiracy content. It just knows which one people click on more. And it serves more of whichever one keeps you scrolling.

Paul described this dynamic with remarkable precision in 2 Timothy 4:3-4. "The time will come when they will not endure sound doctrine, but according to their own desires, because they have itching ears, they will heap up for themselves teachers; and they will turn their ears away from the truth, and be turned aside to fables." Itching ears. That phrase is worth sitting with. An itch demands scratching. It's not a considered desire. It's a compulsive one. And the person with itching ears doesn't go looking for what's true. They go looking for what feels satisfying, for what confirms what they already suspect, for what gives them the feeling of being informed, awake, and ahead of the crowd. The algorithm is extraordinarily good at finding those people and feeding them exactly what their ears are itching for.

The result is what's been called radicalization, and it happens to people who would never describe themselves as radical. A believer who would never attend a fringe church, who would never follow a cult leader, who genuinely loves God and their family and their local congregation, can nonetheless be slowly shaped by months and years of online content into someone who thinks in ways that are increasingly disconnected from Scripture, from their pastor's teaching, and from the ordinary wisdom of the believing community around them. It doesn't happen all at once. It happens the same way the frog in the gradually heating water doesn't notice the temperature rising. Each piece of content is just a little more extreme than the last. Each teacher is just a little more certain, a little more urgent, a little more willing to make claims that more careful voices won't make. And because the algorithm keeps serving content that matches what you've already engaged with, the world you see through your screen gradually narrows until the only voices you're hearing are the ones that agree with each other, reinforce each other, and collectively create the impression that what they're saying is simply obvious reality that everyone else is too blind or too compromised to see.

That's an echo chamber. And it's one of the most spiritually dangerous environments a Christian can inhabit, precisely because it feels like the opposite of danger. It feels like clarity. It feels like finally seeing what's really going on. It feels like being part of a community of people who are awake when everyone else is asleep. That feeling is one of the most powerful psychological pulls fanaticism offers, and the digital world has made it available to anyone with a smartphone and a Wi-Fi connection.

The psychological dynamics underneath this are worth understanding, because understanding them helps you recognize when they're operating in you. The first is the appeal of special knowledge. There's a genuine psychological reward that comes from feeling like you know something others don't. It produces a sense of significance, of purpose, of being part of something important. The problem is that this reward is available regardless of whether the knowledge is actually true. The feeling of being an insider, of having access to information that the mainstream is hiding or ignoring, is pleasurable independent of the accuracy of the information. And that pleasure can become a kind of addiction, driving a constant search for the next piece of hidden truth that produces the next hit of insider significance.

The second dynamic is the anxiety cycle. Fear-based content produces anxiety. Anxiety drives more consumption, because the anxious person keeps looking for information that will resolve the anxiety. But fear-based content doesn't resolve anxiety. It feeds it. Each new piece of alarming information produces more anxiety, which produces more consumption, which produces more anxiety, in a loop that can run for years without ever reaching the resolution it promises. The person caught in this cycle often doesn't realize they're in it. They experience the consumption as necessary, as responsible, as what a faithful watchman does. But the fruit of the cycle is not faithfulness. It's a chronic low-grade fear that colors everything, erodes joy, and makes genuine rest in God feel almost impossible.

The third dynamic is the erosion of trust in local community. This is perhaps the most damaging long-term effect of the digital echo chamber. When someone's primary spiritual formation is happening through online content rather than through a local church community, their relationship to that community gradually changes. The pastor's teaching starts to feel insufficient compared to the depth and urgency of what they're consuming online. The small group conversations start to feel shallow. The other believers around them start to seem uninformed, spiritually asleep, or unwilling to take seriously what the person has been learning. The community that God designed to be the primary context for spiritual growth, accountability, and mutual care slowly gets replaced by a digital community of people who share the same content and reinforce the same conclusions. And that digital community, unlike a real local church, has no ability to know you, challenge you, or hold you accountable in the ways that genuine community requires.

Paul's instruction in 2 Timothy 2:23-25 is the antidote to all of this. "Avoid foolish and ignorant disputes, knowing that they generate strife. And a servant of the Lord must not quarrel but be gentle to all, able to teach, patient, in humility correcting those who are in opposition." Gentle to all. Patient. Humble. Those words describe a person who is not living in an echo chamber, because echo chambers don't produce gentleness. They produce the opposite. They produce a person who is increasingly confident in their own position, increasingly impatient with those who don't share it, and increasingly inclined to see opposition as evidence of the opponent's spiritual failure rather than as an opportunity for humble engagement.

The digital world isn't going away. The question isn't whether to engage with it but how to engage with it in a way that doesn't slowly reshape your soul into something that looks less and less like the fruit of the Spirit and more and more like the profile of fanaticism. That requires active, specific choices. Not vague intentions to be more careful. Actual decisions about what you consume, how much you consume it, and what you do with the space you create by consuming less of it.

Guarding your digital consumption is a spiritual discipline. It belongs in the same category as prayer, fasting, and Scripture reading. Not because technology is evil, but because the soul is shaped by what it consistently takes in, and the digital environment is specifically designed by very intelligent people to maximize your consumption of whatever keeps you most engaged. Your engagement and your spiritual formation are not the same thing. Often they're in direct conflict. Recognizing that conflict and making deliberate choices in light of it is part of what it means to live as a stranger in a culture that has made constant connectivity feel like a virtue.

Guardrails for Discernment

You need a practical framework for evaluating the competing spiritual voices that are constantly competing for your attention. Not a vague commitment to "be more discerning." A specific set of questions you can actually apply to a specific teacher, a specific message, or a specific movement. The following five questions are designed to do exactly that. They're not exhaustive, but they're enough. If you apply them honestly to any teaching you're considering, they'll tell you what you need to know.

The first question is: does this teaching center on Christ, or does it center on threats and enemies?

This is the most fundamental question, and it's worth spending real time on. A Christ-centered teaching keeps returning to who Jesus is, what He accomplished, and what His life, death, and resurrection mean for how we live right now. It uses current events, cultural analysis, and prophetic insight in service of a deeper encounter with Christ. An enemy-centered teaching uses Christ primarily as the authority behind the warning about the threat. The threat is the main event. Christ is the credential. These two postures produce very different spiritual conditions in the people who receive them. One produces worship. The other produces surveillance. When you're evaluating a teacher or a message, ask yourself honestly: after spending time with this content, am I more focused on Christ or more focused on the enemy? The answer tells you where the teaching's center of gravity actually is, regardless of how much Jesus-language it uses.

The second question is: does this teaching produce love for people, including opponents, or does it produce contempt?

Pay attention to how a teacher talks about people who disagree with them. Do they engage opposing views with genuine respect, even while disagreeing clearly? Or do they dismiss, mock, or impugn the motives of anyone who doesn't share their position? And pay attention to what the teaching produces in you. After consuming this content, do you find yourself more patient with the people around you, more genuinely caring about people who hold different views? Or do you find yourself more irritated, more suspicious, more inclined to categorize people as either awake or asleep, as either part of the solution or part of the problem? The emotional temperature that a teaching produces in you is data. It's telling you something about the spirit behind the teaching. Love, by definition, includes opponents. A teaching that produces contempt for opponents, no matter how doctrinally sophisticated it is, has failed the most basic test Paul sets in 1 Corinthians 13.

The third question is: does this teaching require secret knowledge available only to insiders?

The gospel has never been a secret. It was proclaimed publicly, in synagogues and marketplaces and temple courts, to anyone who would listen. It didn't require special initiation or insider access. When a teaching begins to position itself as knowledge that the mainstream church is hiding, suppressing, or too spiritually blind to see, that positioning itself is a warning sign. It's not that genuine prophetic insight is never countercultural or unpopular. It sometimes is. The prophets of the Old Testament were frequently unwelcome. But there's a difference between a message that's unpopular because it calls people to costly faithfulness and a message that's positioned as secret because the secrecy is part of its appeal. The first kind of prophetic voice says, "Here is what God has said clearly in Scripture, and it calls us to something difficult." The second says, "Here is what they don't want you to know." The first serves the community. The second serves the ego of the insider.

The fourth question is: does this teaching bear the fruit of the Spirit in the people who follow it?

This is the Matthew 7 test applied practically. You're not just looking at the teacher. You're looking at the people who've been shaped by the teaching over time. Are they more loving than they were before they encountered this content? More patient? More gentle? More rooted in their local church community? More genuinely present to the people immediately around them? Or are they more anxious, more isolated, more suspicious, more certain of their own spiritual superiority, and more disconnected from the ordinary life of the local church? The fruit of the followers is as telling as the fruit of the teacher. A tree is known by its fruit. A teaching is known by the people it produces.

The fifth question is: is this teacher accountable to a local church body?

This one is specific and practical, and it matters more than most people realize. A teacher who operates entirely outside of local church accountability, who answers to no elders, no congregation, no community of believers who know them personally and can speak honestly into their life and their ministry, is operating without one of the most important safeguards God built into the church. Local church accountability doesn't guarantee that a teacher is right about everything. But its absence removes a significant check on the kind of uncorrected certainty that fanaticism requires to grow. The teachers who've done the most damage in church history have almost always been operating outside of genuine accountability structures. That's not a coincidence. Accountability is uncomfortable precisely because it requires you to be known, to be questioned, and to be correctable. A teacher who has arranged their ministry so that they can never be corrected has arranged their ministry so that they can never be corrected. That's not a safe place to receive spiritual formation from.

These five questions work together. A teaching that passes all five isn't guaranteed to be right about everything. But a teaching that fails even one of them deserves serious caution. And a teaching that fails multiple of them deserves to be set down entirely, regardless of how compelling it feels in the moment, regardless of how urgent it claims to be, and regardless of how many other people seem to be following it.

The difference between a prophetic warning and a divisive controversy is worth naming directly, because fanaticism always presents itself as the former. A prophetic warning calls people to repentance, to holiness, to faithfulness, and to love. It centers on Christ. It produces humility in the person who receives it. It draws people into deeper dependence on God and deeper commitment to the community of believers. A divisive controversy, by contrast, centers on the controversy itself. It produces pride in those who understand it and contempt for those who don't. It pulls people away from their local church and toward an online community of people who share the same concerns. It generates more heat than light, more strife than holiness, more separation than unity. Titus 3:9-11 is clear about how to handle someone who keeps generating divisive controversy: warn them once, warn them a second time, and then withdraw. Not because the issues don't matter, but because a person committed to division has already decided that the controversy matters more than the community. And a community that keeps engaging that person on their terms will eventually be shaped by those terms.

Navigating this landscape requires the kind of settled, Christ-centered confidence that doesn't need the latest revelation to feel spiritually alive. The person who is genuinely rooted in Scripture, genuinely connected to a local church community, genuinely formed by the ordinary means of grace, that person is actually quite difficult to radicalize. Not because they're closed-minded, but because they have a reference point that's stable enough to measure new claims against. The echo chamber only works on people who have no other significant source of formation to push back against it. Rootedness in a real community, under real pastoral care, with real accountability, is one of the most powerful defenses against fanaticism that exists. It's not glamorous. It's not exciting. But it works.

Marks of Maturity: Recap and Action Steps

The contrast between fanaticism and gospel maturity can be stated simply. Fanaticism is marked by urgency without love, certainty without humility, a fixation on enemies, contempt for opponents, and the neglect of ordinary faithfulness in favor of spectacular claims. Gospel maturity is marked by love, joy, peace, patience, kindness, goodness, faithfulness, gentleness, and self-control. None of those nine qualities are dramatic. All of them are evidence of the Spirit's actual presence.

The call of this book has been consistent from the first chapter. Holy defiance isn't primarily about what you're against. It's about who you belong to, and how that belonging reshapes every part of how you live. The stranger in a culture of compromise isn't the loudest voice in the room. They're the most genuinely different person in the room. Different in their patience. Different in their peace. Different in their willingness to love people that the surrounding culture has decided are enemies. That kind of difference is the most powerful witness the church has ever had, and it's the kind that fanaticism actively destroys.

The following action steps are specific. They're designed to move you from wherever you are right now toward the kind of sober, rooted, love-producing faith this chapter has been describing.

First: Do a specific audit of your digital consumption this week. Go through your phone and identify every account, channel, podcast, or website that regularly produces anxiety, outrage, or a sense of insider knowledge about spiritual threats. Write them down. Don't rationalize any of them. Just list them. Then apply the five discernment questions to each one. If a source fails two or more of the five questions, unfollow or unsubscribe from it today. Not eventually. Today. This is a concrete action with a concrete outcome: a digital environment that is measurably less shaped by fanatical content. It will feel like a loss at first. That feeling is worth paying attention to. It's telling you how much of your spiritual attention that content had claimed.

Second: Commit to one week of digital silence on all speculative spiritual content. For seven consecutive days, consume no prophecy news, no end-times commentary, no "what's really going on" spiritual analysis online. None. Replace that time with something specific: fifteen minutes of reading in the Gospels each day, paying attention only to what Jesus actually said and did. Not what a teacher says Jesus meant. What the text says. At the end of the seven days, write down three specific things you noticed about Jesus in those readings that you hadn't been paying attention to. The exercise isn't about condemning the content you stopped consuming. It's about discovering what fills the space when that content is absent. Most people who do this discover that the silence is uncomfortable for the first two or three days and then something settles. The anxiety level drops. The sense of threat recedes. And the actual presence of God, accessible through His Word and through prayer, becomes more real and more available than it had been in a long time.

Third: Have one honest conversation with your pastor or a trusted elder this month about something you've been consuming online that has been shaping your thinking. Not to get permission. Not to confess a sin. To submit your spiritual diet to someone who knows you, loves you, and is accountable to God for your care. Describe specifically what you've been watching or reading. Ask them honestly: does this look healthy to you? Does this seem consistent with what you're seeing in me? That conversation might be uncomfortable. It's supposed to be. Accountability is uncomfortable because it requires you to be known. But the discomfort of being known is infinitely safer than the comfort of an echo chamber that shapes you in ways no one around you can see or speak into.

Fourth: Choose one person in your life who holds a different theological or political view than you, and do one specific act of genuine kindness toward them this week. Not a debate. Not an attempt to correct them. A genuine act of care. Bring them a meal. Help them with something practical. Send them a message that has nothing to do with your disagreements and everything to do with the fact that you actually care about them as a person. This is the love test applied in practice. It's easy to say you love people who disagree with you. It's much harder to actually serve them. The act of service does something to your heart that argument can't do. It's very difficult to maintain contempt for someone you've just helped. And contempt, as we've seen, is one of the clearest signs that fanaticism has taken root. Kindness is the weed killer.

The fruit of the Spirit is the test. It has always been the test. And it's the one test that fanaticism, with all its urgency and certainty and insider knowledge, consistently fails. The person who is genuinely walking in love, joy, peace, patience, kindness, goodness, faithfulness, gentleness, and self-control is already doing the most countercultural thing a human being can do in this moment. They don't need a prophecy chart to be a witness. Their life is the witness. And that witness, quiet and unspectacular as it may seem, is exactly what the world around them has no category for and no explanation of. That's the holy defiance this book has been pointing toward all along.

8

WHEN WORSHIP LOOKS LIKE EGYPT

Aaron didn't introduce a foreign god. That's the part of the story that most people miss when they read Exodus 32. He took gold from the people, fashioned a calf, and then declared, "This is your god, O Israel, who brought you up out of the land of Egypt." And then he announced a feast to the Lord. He used God's name. He credited God's deliverance. He organized a religious gathering. By almost every outward measure, what happened at the foot of Sinai looked like worship. It just wasn't. The name was right. The form was borrowed from Egypt. And that combination turned out to be one of the most dangerous things God's people have ever done.

That's syncretism at its most subtle. Not a flat rejection of God. A repackaging of Him into something the surrounding culture would recognize and feel comfortable with.

The reason this story matters so much right now is that the same pattern is alive and running in thousands of churches across the Western world. Not because pastors are secretly pagans. Not because believers have consciously decided to abandon biblical worship. But because the pressure to make worship accessible, culturally relevant, and emotionally satisfying has slowly pulled the form of corporate worship away from what God actually commands and toward what the surrounding entertainment culture expects. And most people sitting in those services don't notice, because the name of Jesus is still being used. The lights are on. The music is loud. The atmosphere feels spiritual. It just isn't always the Spirit.

The Golden Calf Pattern

To understand what went wrong at Sinai, you have to understand what Aaron was actually doing. Egypt had a rich visual culture of religious worship. Animals were sacred. Images were central. The gods were made visible, touchable, present. When Israel had been in Egypt for four hundred years, that way of relating to the divine had gotten deep into their bones. Moses had been on the mountain for forty days, and the people were anxious. They wanted something they could see. Something familiar. Something that felt like God was actually there.

So Aaron gave them what Egypt had taught them to want.

The calf wasn't a rejection of the God who brought them out of Egypt. Aaron's declaration made that clear. It was a redefinition of how that God should be approached. Instead of the invisible, holy, sovereign God who spoke from fire and cloud and required specific, careful, reverent worship on His own terms, they got a visible, manageable, aesthetically satisfying representation they could relate to on their own terms. The worship was still pointed in God's direction. But the form had been imported from the culture they were supposed to be leaving behind.

Nadab and Abihu, Aaron's own sons, repeated a version of the same error in Leviticus 10. They offered what the text calls "strange fire before the Lord, which He had not commanded them." The fire was real fire. The altar was the right altar. The setting was correct. But the worship was unauthorized. It was fire offered on their own terms rather than God's. And God's response was immediate and devastating. He consumed them where they stood. Then He said something to Aaron that cuts through every casual approach to worship: "I will be sanctified by those who come near Me."

God doesn't say, "I appreciate the effort." He says, "I will be treated as holy by the people who approach Me." The how of worship matters to God. Not just the who.

This is the pattern that runs from the golden calf through Nadab and Abihu and straight into the present. It isn't primarily about people who hate God or want to abandon Him. It's about people who love God, who genuinely want to worship Him, but who have allowed the surrounding culture to define what that worship looks like. They've kept the name. They've borrowed the form. And the result is worship that looks and feels religious while being shaped by something other than God's own self-revelation.

The modern version of this pattern shows up most clearly in what's been called celebrity worship culture in the church. When the draw of a Sunday gathering is the personality of the worship leader or the charisma of the pastor rather than the presence of Christ, the golden calf pattern is being replicated. The leader becomes the visible, accessible, emotionally compelling representation of God. The congregation's connection is to the person on stage rather than to the Lord. This isn't primarily the leader's fault. It's a systemic issue rooted in a culture that has been trained by decades of entertainment media to relate to personalities rather than to truth. The church absorbed that training without fully realizing it. And now many congregations have, functionally, a golden calf with a guitar and a good speaking voice.

The severity of God's response to unauthorized worship in the Old Testament isn't meant to produce fear for its own sake. It's meant to produce an honest reckoning with a question most Christians have never seriously asked: what does God actually want when His people gather? Not what feels good. Not what draws a crowd. Not what makes people feel spiritually satisfied for an hour on Sunday morning. What does God want? That question, asked honestly and answered from Scripture rather than from cultural expectation, is where the reformation of worship has to begin.

Spectacle vs. Substance

Before going further, something needs to be said clearly to prevent a misreading that would miss the point entirely. This chapter isn't an argument against contemporary music, good lighting, or modern aesthetics in worship. The issue has nothing to do with whether your church uses a hymnal or a screen, an organ or a band, a traditional liturgy or a more spontaneous format. A hymn sung in a cathedral can be just as self-centered as a concert-style performance if the heart behind it is about tradition and respectability rather than encountering the living God. The form isn't the problem. The orientation is.

The diagnostic question isn't "what style is this?" It's "who is this for?"

That question cuts through all the surface-level debates about worship style and gets to the thing that actually matters. A worship service designed primarily around the emotional experience of the people attending it is a fundamentally different thing from a worship service designed primarily around the self-revelation of God. Both can use the same songs. Both can have the same order of service. But they're doing completely different things to the people who participate in them. One is shaping people to be consumers of spiritual experience. The other is shaping people to be worshippers of a holy God.

Concert culture has given the church a powerful set of tools for producing emotional responses in large groups of people. Lighting design, musical dynamics, carefully sequenced song sets that build emotional energy toward a climactic moment, the charismatic presence of a skilled communicator, all of these things are genuinely effective at generating feelings of transcendence, connection, and spiritual warmth. The problem is that those feelings can be generated entirely without the actual presence of the Holy Spirit. And when a congregation is trained to equate those feelings with God's presence, they lose the ability to tell the difference between atmosphere and encounter.

Think about what happens to a person who has spent years in that kind of environment. They arrive at church already calibrated to receive an emotional experience. If the music is good, if the atmosphere is right, if the speaker is engaging, they leave feeling that worship happened. If the band had an off night, if the speaker was less compelling than usual, if the lighting felt flat, they leave feeling like worship didn't quite happen. Their sense of God's presence has become entirely dependent on external production values. They've been trained, without anyone intending it, to locate God in the atmosphere rather than in His Word and in the gathered community of His people.

That's not a small problem. It's actually a form of spiritual dependency that leaves people unable to worship when the production isn't there. They can't encounter God in silence. They can't pray without background music. They can't find Him in the ordinary, unspectacular reading of Scripture without someone making it feel dramatic. Egypt taught them to need the golden calf. And now they can't imagine worship without one.

Consider a hypothetical person like Marcus, a 37-year-old worship pastor who genuinely loves God and has given years of his life to leading people into His presence. He's gifted. He works hard. He cares deeply about what happens on Sunday mornings. But over time, without fully realizing it, he's started measuring the success of a service by the emotional peak it produced. He adjusts song keys to maximize singability. He sequences sets to build toward a moment of emotional release. He watches the congregation's body language to gauge whether they're "in it." He's not doing anything cynical. He's doing what he was trained to do and what the culture around him rewards. But the thing he's been optimizing for is emotional response, not encounter with God. And those two things are not the same. Sometimes they overlap. But they can be completely separated. And in a culture that's been trained to mistake one for the other, that separation is one of the most spiritually dangerous things that can happen in a church.

The return to substance over spectacle isn't a call to make worship boring, cold, or emotionally flat. God is worthy of the best music, the most careful preparation, the deepest engagement of every human faculty. Reverence and beauty aren't opposites. Awe isn't the same thing as boredom. What the return to substance requires is a reorientation of the question driving every worship decision. Not "will this move people?" but "does this reflect who God actually is?" Not "will this keep people engaged?" but "does this open people to genuine encounter with the living God?" Those questions lead to different choices. They lead to worship that takes the Word of God seriously as the primary vehicle of God's self-revelation. They lead to prayer that's honest rather than performed. They lead to a gathering where the presence of the Holy Spirit is the thing being sought, not the thing being simulated.

Reverence and awe aren't museum pieces from a previous era of church history. They're the appropriate response to a God who told His people that He will be treated as holy by those who come near Him. That standard didn't expire with the Old Testament. It's the permanent condition of approaching the God of Scripture. And a worship culture that has lost its sense of awe, that treats Sunday morning as a spiritual pep rally rather than a holy gathering before a holy God, has lost something that can't be replaced by better production values or more engaging speakers.

The Liturgy of Desire

Every church service has a liturgy. That word doesn't belong only to high-church traditions with robes and chanted prayers. It belongs to every gathering, because every gathering has an order, a rhythm, a sequence of events that shapes the people who participate in it. The question isn't whether your church has a liturgy. It's what your church's liturgy is actually doing to the people who experience it week after week.

The philosopher James K.A. Smith made an observation that's worth sitting with. He argued that our desires are shaped by our practices before they're shaped by our beliefs. You don't first decide what to want and then find practices that reflect those desires. You practice certain things repeatedly, and those practices gradually form what you want. The rhythms of your daily and weekly life are quietly shaping your heart's orientation, your imagination, your sense of what's normal, what's satisfying, and what you're moving toward. That's true of everything from your morning routine to your social media habits to the way your church service is structured.

A worship service that's designed to build emotional energy toward a climactic musical moment, with the sermon functioning as an interlude between song sets, has a liturgy. And that liturgy is forming people. It's teaching them, week after week, that the high point of encountering God is an emotional peak produced by music. It's training their desires toward experience. It's shaping them to be consumers of spiritual feeling rather than worshippers who engage with God through His Word, respond in repentance and faith, and are sent out into the world with a mission. The liturgy of a consumer-oriented service produces consumers. Not disciples. And the tragedy is that it does this to people who are genuinely trying to worship God. The form is shaping them in ways they haven't chosen and often can't see.

A service structured around the Word of God looks different. Not necessarily less beautiful or less emotionally engaging. But the arc is different. The gathering begins with a recognition of who God is, drawn from Scripture rather than from the band's energy. The confession of sin is real rather than perfunctory, because a God who is actually holy requires actual repentance from people who are actually broken. The Scripture is read carefully and taught seriously, not as a launching pad for motivational content but as the actual living voice of God speaking into the room. The response to the Word comes in prayer, in communion, in giving, in commitment. And the people are sent out with a clear understanding that the worship they've just participated in is connected to the life they're about to live for the next six days.

That kind of liturgy forms disciples. It trains desire toward God Himself rather than toward an experience of God. It shapes people to want what God wants rather than to want what the surrounding culture has trained them to want. And it does this not primarily through instruction but through repetition. The rhythm of gathering, hearing, responding, and being sent becomes the rhythm of a life that's oriented toward God rather than toward self.

The practical question this raises is one that requires genuine honesty: what is the liturgy of your church actually forming you to desire? After a year of attending your current church, are you more hungry for God's Word? More convicted by sin? More genuinely prayerful in your daily life? More shaped by a sense of mission? Or are you more dependent on a particular worship experience to feel spiritually alive? More drawn to the next conference, the next special speaker, the next powerful service? More reliant on emotional peaks to confirm that God is present? Those questions aren't meant to produce guilt. They're meant to produce clarity. Because if the liturgy of your church is forming you to desire an experience rather than to behold God, that's not a small thing. It's the golden calf pattern operating through the structure of your weekly worship rather than through a physical idol.

The call back to biblical worship is a call back to the shape that the New Testament actually describes for the gathered church. First Corinthians 14 describes a gathering where everything is done for edification, where the Word is central, where everyone participates in a way that builds up the body. Colossians 3:16 says to "let the word of Christ dwell in you richly, teaching and admonishing one another in all wisdom, singing psalms and hymns and spiritual songs." The music in that description is in service of the Word dwelling richly. The Word is the thing. The music serves it. That order matters. When it gets reversed, when the music is the thing and the Word serves the atmosphere, the liturgy has been inverted. And an inverted liturgy produces an inverted faith.

None of this is meant to produce despair about the state of the church. God is at work in congregations across the entire spectrum of worship styles, and His Spirit is not limited by poor production choices or misguided service structures. But the call of this book has been consistent from the beginning: holy defiance means refusing to let the surrounding culture define what faithfulness looks like. That call applies to worship as much as it applies to money, politics, or entertainment. The world has a very clear idea of what a compelling gathering looks like. It looks like a concert. It looks like a TED talk. It looks like an emotionally satisfying experience designed to make you feel good about yourself and your choices. The church isn't called to produce that. The church is called to produce something the world has no category for: a gathering of broken people before a holy God, shaped by His Word, responding in genuine faith, and sent out to live differently than everyone around them. That gathering might not look impressive by the world's standards. But it's the only kind of gathering that actually produces what God is after.

Returning to What Matters: Reflection and Next Steps

The warning against unauthorized worship isn't abstract theology. It's a live issue for every believer who participates in corporate worship, which means it's a live issue for you. The golden calf pattern doesn't require bad intentions. It requires only that the surrounding culture's expectations be allowed to shape worship more than God's Word does. And in a culture saturated with entertainment, celebrity, and emotional experience, that drift happens easily and quietly, one service at a time.

The following steps are specific. They're designed to move you from awareness to actual reorientation, starting this week.

First: Before your next church service, spend ten minutes in silent prayer with no music, no phone, and no preparation of any kind except this one question: "God, what do you want to say to me today?" Not "what do I want to get out of this service?" Not "I hope the music is good." Just that one question, held in silence for ten minutes. Write down whatever comes to mind. Then go to the service. Afterward, compare what you wrote down with what actually happened in the gathering. This practice does two things. It reorients your posture from consumer to worshipper before you walk through the door. And it begins to train you to bring expectation toward God's self-revelation rather than toward the service's production quality. Do this for four consecutive Sundays and pay attention to how your experience of the gathering changes.

Second: Honestly evaluate the liturgy of your current church using three specific questions. Write your answers down rather than just thinking through them. Question one: in a typical service, what is the high point? Is it a musical moment, a compelling personal story from the speaker, or an encounter with the text of Scripture? Question two: after a year of attending this church, are you more hungry for God's Word on your own, or more dependent on the Sunday experience to feel spiritually connected? Question three: does the structure of the service send you out with a clear sense of mission, or does it primarily leave you feeling emotionally satisfied? Your honest answers to those three questions will tell you what the liturgy has been forming in you. If the answers concern you, that's not a reason to leave your church. It's a reason to pray specifically for your church's leadership, and to take personal responsibility for what's forming you outside of Sunday morning.

Third: Identify one specific way you've been treating atmosphere as a substitute for the actual presence of God. Be specific. Maybe you can't pray without background music. Maybe you only feel close to God at conferences or special services. Maybe you've stopped reading Scripture on your own because it feels flat without someone making it feel compelling. Whatever it is, name it in one specific sentence. Then for the next two weeks, do the opposite of that habit once per day. Pray in complete silence. Read one chapter of Scripture with no music, no commentary, no preparation, just you and the text. Sit in stillness before God for five minutes with nothing happening. The discomfort you feel is important information. It's showing you how dependent your sense of God's presence has become on external conditions He never promised to require. The goal isn't to make worship feel harder. The goal is to rediscover that God is present in the ordinary, unspectacular, unproduced encounter with His Word and His Spirit.

Finally: Ask God one honest question and write down the answer. The question is this: "In the way I've been worshipping you, have I been coming to you on your terms or on mine?" Sit with that question for at least fifteen minutes. Don't rush to an answer that makes you feel okay. Let the honest answer surface. Write it down. If what comes up reveals that your worship has been more about what you get from it than about who God is, that's not condemnation. That's the beginning of the kind of reorientation that this entire chapter has been pointing toward. Worship that's genuinely oriented toward God's glory rather than personal experience is the most countercultural thing a person can do in a world that has made self-satisfaction the measure of everything. It's also the most transformative. And it starts with the willingness to ask the question honestly and sit with whatever the answer turns out to be.

The golden calf at Sinai was built by people who genuinely wanted to worship God. That's what makes the story so sobering and so relevant. The danger isn't primarily in the hearts of people who don't care about God. It's in the habits of people who do care but have allowed Egypt's forms to shape how they express that care. Coming out of Egypt, as this book has been arguing from the beginning, means more than changing your theology or your politics or your spending habits. It means examining the very shape of your worship and asking whether what you're doing on Sunday morning is drawing you toward the holy, living God of Scripture or toward a more comfortable, culturally familiar version of Him. The difference between those two things is the difference between the golden calf and the burning bush. One is what we make when we're anxious and Egypt is still in us. The other is what God offers when we've traveled far enough from Egypt to hear Him speak.

9

THE HEART OF TRUE WORSHIP

Chapter 8 exposed what worship looks like when Egypt's forms have infiltrated the gathered church. This chapter turns in a different direction. If the previous chapter diagnosed the problem, this one describes what's actually healthy. And the picture Scripture paints is far bigger, far more demanding, and far more freeing than most Christians have been taught to expect.

Most believers have been handed a definition of worship that's roughly this size: an hour on Sunday morning where you sing songs to God. Maybe you'd expand it to include personal devotions, prayer, and the occasional conference. But the core picture is still event-shaped. Worship is something you do at a specific time, in a specific place, and then you go back to regular life until the next one.

That picture is too small. And the smallness of it is costing people something they can't fully name.

When worship gets reduced to an event, the rest of life gets handed over to whatever values the surrounding culture supplies. Monday through Saturday runs on the world's operating system while Sunday gets a brief override. The gap between those two realities is exactly what produces the hollow feeling so many sincere believers carry. They're not hypocrites. They're not walking away from God. They've just inherited a definition of worship that's too narrow to hold their whole life, and so their whole life never gets offered.

Romans 12:1 is where this chapter begins. Paul writes: "I beseech you therefore, brethren, by the mercies of God, that you present your bodies a living sacrifice, holy, acceptable to God, which is your reasonable service." That phrase "reasonable service" is worth slowing down on. In the original Greek, Paul uses the word logikēn latreian. The word latreia is temple language. It's the same word used for priestly service in the Old Testament sanctuary. Paul is doing something deliberate and startling here. He's taking the vocabulary of the temple, the vocabulary of priests and altars and sacred offerings, and applying it to the bodies of ordinary believers going about ordinary life. Your body, he says, is now the temple. Your daily existence is now the priestly service. Every act of obedience is now the offering on the altar.

That's not a metaphor meant to make you feel good. It's a theological statement that rewrites the entire map of what worship is.

The Living Sacrifice Framework

A dead sacrifice stays on the altar. That's what made the old system manageable. You brought your animal. It died. The offering was complete. You went home. But Paul doesn't call believers dead sacrifices. He calls them living ones. And a living sacrifice has a problem that a dead one doesn't have.

It keeps crawling off.

That's not a criticism. It's just the honest reality of what whole-life worship actually requires. The daily challenge isn't a single dramatic moment of consecration where you surrender everything and then you're done. It's a repeated, moment-by-moment return to the altar. Your time crawls off the altar and gets spent on things that serve only you. Your attention crawls off and gets absorbed by whatever your phone is offering. Your words crawl off and start serving your ego instead of your neighbor. Your money crawls off toward comfort and status. Your ambitions crawl off toward self-advancement. And the work of worship, real worship, is the daily discipline of climbing back up and saying again, "This belongs to God."

That reframing changes everything about how you approach an ordinary Tuesday.

Think about what this means practically. Consider a hypothetical 36-year-old named Grace, a school teacher and mother of two who genuinely loves God but has quietly felt for years that her faith only really counts during church services and personal devotions. The rest of her life, the lesson planning, the parent-teacher conferences, the school lunches she packs, the homework she helps with at the kitchen table, all of that has felt like the secular part of her week. The ordinary part. The part that doesn't quite qualify as spiritual. What Romans 12:1 says to Grace is that she's been wrong about that. Every lesson she prepares with genuine care for her students is a priestly offering. Every moment she parents with patience when she's exhausted is a sacrifice placed on the altar. Every conversation she has with a struggling parent, handled with honesty and kindness, is worship in the fullest sense of the word latreia.

This isn't a new idea. The Reformers, particularly Luther, recovered it in the sixteenth century when they pushed back against the idea that only priests and monks were doing truly holy work. Luther argued that every legitimate calling, the farmer, the merchant, the parent, the magistrate, is a form of service to God when done in faith and love. A carpenter who frames a house with integrity is performing priestly service. A nurse who cares for a dying patient with genuine compassion is standing at the altar. That vision didn't originate with

Luther. It was always in the text. He just cleared away the centuries of religious hierarchy that had buried it.

The division between sacred work and secular work is itself a distortion. It has roots in Greek philosophy, which separated the spiritual from the physical, the eternal from the ordinary. That division got absorbed into certain strands of Christian thinking and produced the idea that real holiness belongs to monks and clergy while ordinary people do ordinary things. But that's not the world the New Testament describes. First Peter 2:5 says that believers are "living stones" being built into a spiritual house, a holy priesthood, offering up spiritual sacrifices. Not some believers. All of them. The priesthood of all believers isn't just a theological slogan about access to God in prayer. It's a statement about the worshipful nature of every believer's entire life when it's offered to God.

Micah 6:6-8 cuts through any remaining confusion about what God is actually after. The people in Micah's day were asking what kind of offering would satisfy God. Thousands of rams? Rivers of oil? Their firstborn children? The offerings kept getting bigger, more impressive, more dramatic. And God's answer through Micah was devastating in its simplicity. "What does the Lord require of you but to do justly, to love mercy, and to walk humbly with your God?" Three things. Not a sacrifice count. Not a religious performance score. Justice, mercy, and humility, lived out in the texture of daily relationships, daily decisions, daily interactions with other people. Worship that doesn't produce those qualities in your actual life isn't worship. It's religious activity with the soul taken out.

Hebrews 13:15-16 holds both sides of this together in a single breath. "A sacrifice of praise, the fruit of lips that confess His name, and doing good and sharing, for with such sacrifices God is well pleased." The sacrifice of praise belongs alongside doing good and sharing. The verbal and the practical. The gathered and the scattered. Both are worship. Both please God. Neither is complete without the other. The person who sings beautifully on Sunday and treats their employees poorly on Wednesday hasn't worshipped in any sense that Scripture recognizes. The person who is generous and just in their daily life but never gathers with the body of Christ to confess His name together has also missed something essential. The living sacrifice framework holds these together. Your whole life, gathered and scattered, private and public, is the offering.

James 1:27 says it plainly: "Pure and undefiled religion before God and the Father is this: to visit orphans and widows in their affliction, and to keep oneself unspotted from the world." Two things. Active care for the vulnerable and personal holiness. Both are religion in the truest sense. Not as alternatives to gathered worship but as the shape that genuine worship takes when it spills out of Sunday and into the rest of the week. When your worship is only ever an event, it can't produce this. When your worship is a life, it can't help but produce it.

The practical implication of all this is that you don't need a more intense Sunday experience to become a deeper worshipper. You need a more intentional Monday. You need to begin seeing the ordinary tasks of your calling, your work, your parenting, your relationships, your stewardship of money and time, as the altar on which your daily offering is placed. That reorientation doesn't make Sunday less important. It makes it the gathering point where the whole-life offering gets expressed together with other believers, celebrated, renewed, and sent back out into the world. Sunday becomes the summit rather than the substitute.

The Altar of Brokenness

There's a moment in Psalm 51 that stops you if you read it slowly enough. David has sinned catastrophically. He's committed adultery with Bathsheba. He's arranged the murder of her husband Uriah to cover it up. The prophet Nathan has confronted him and the full weight of what he's done has landed on him. And in the middle of his prayer of repentance, he says something that cuts against every instinct toward religious self-improvement: "You do not desire sacrifice, or else I would give it; You do not delight in burnt offering. The sacrifices of God are a broken spirit, a broken and a contrite heart, these, O God, You will not despise."

David knew the sacrificial system. He knew what the Law required. He could have gone through every prescribed ritual. He could have offered every appropriate animal. And he's saying that none of that is what God actually wants from him in this moment. What God wants is the broken heart underneath all the religious activity.

The Hebrew word translated "contrite" in that verse is dakka. It means crushed. Pulverized. Ground to powder. It's the opposite of self-sufficiency. It's the opposite of religious pride. A contrite heart isn't one that feels vaguely sorry and hopes things will improve. It's one that has been completely stripped of the pretense that it has something to offer God on its own terms. It comes with nothing. It brings no credentials, no track record, no argument for why it deserves mercy. It just comes crushed, and it trusts that God will not despise what it's bringing.

Jesus said almost exactly the same thing in the first beatitude. "Blessed are the poor in spirit, for theirs is the kingdom of heaven." Poor in spirit. That phrase describes someone who has nothing in the spiritual account. No reserves of self-righteousness. No cushion of religious achievement to fall back on. They know they're bankrupt before God, and they've stopped pretending otherwise. And Jesus says that's precisely where the kingdom of heaven belongs to them. Not to the spiritually wealthy. Not to the religiously impressive. To the poor in spirit. To the ones who've stopped performing and started arriving empty.

This is where true worship begins. Not with a great song or a powerful sermon or an emotionally charged atmosphere. It begins with the honest acknowledgment that you have nothing to bring that God needs, and everything you have comes from Him anyway. That acknowledgment, made genuinely rather than ritually, is the altar that God is actually looking for. And it's the one that's hardest to build in a culture that rewards confidence, performance, and the appearance of having it together.

The pressure to perform spiritually is real. It shows up in how Christians talk about their faith to each other. The tendency to describe your prayer life as more consistent than it is, your faith as stronger than it feels, your struggles as already resolved rather than still ongoing. There's a social grammar in many church environments that rewards spiritual success and makes spiritual poverty feel like something to be ashamed of rather than something to be honest about. That grammar is a direct enemy of the altar of brokenness. It makes the very thing God says He delights in feel like a liability.

David's psalm cuts through that entirely. Here is the greatest king Israel ever had, a man described as being after God's own heart, writing a prayer that begins with the rawest possible admission of failure and ends with the conviction that God's mercy is real enough to meet him there. Not after he cleans himself up. Not after he's demonstrated sufficient remorse. Right there. In the middle of the wreckage. The broken and contrite heart is the offering. And God does not despise it.

This has a specific implication for how you approach worship, both gathered and scattered. The living sacrifice framework from the previous section describes the whole-life offering. But that offering can only be made genuinely from a posture of brokenness. A person who comes to God with a sense of their own spiritual adequacy, who approaches worship as a transaction where they're giving God what He deserves and expecting appropriate blessings in return, has missed the starting point entirely. The altar of brokenness isn't one stop on the way to more advanced worship. It's the foundation that everything else has to be built on.

Practically, this means that repentance isn't a step you complete and move past. It's a posture you maintain. The living sacrifice keeps crawling off the altar, as we said earlier. And the return to the altar always looks like the return David describes in Psalm 51. Not a dramatic performance of remorse. A quiet, honest, specific acknowledgment that you've been running your own agenda again, and a renewed surrender to God's. That prayer, prayed honestly and regularly, is one of the most countercultural acts a believer can engage in. The world rewards self-sufficiency and punishes the appearance of weakness. God says the crushed heart is exactly what He's looking for.

The connection between brokenness and the living sacrifice framework is important. You can't genuinely offer your whole life to God while still protecting your ego from honest examination. The person who wants to worship with their work but not with their failures, who wants to offer their gifts but not their sins, who wants to present their strengths but not their poverty, is still negotiating the terms of the offering. Moses said not a hoof shall be left behind. The altar of brokenness is where you bring the hooves. The parts of yourself you'd rather keep out of sight. The failures you've been managing rather than confessing. The spiritual poverty you've been covering with religious activity. Those things don't disqualify you from worship. They're the very things God says He delights in receiving.

Humility, mercy, and justice, the three things Micah 6:8 says God requires, all flow from this starting point. You can't walk humbly with God if you haven't genuinely acknowledged your need of Him. You can't love mercy if you haven't needed it yourself in a way that went all the way to the bone. You can't do justice from a posture of self-righteousness. The altar of brokenness isn't just the beginning of worship. It's the thing that keeps every other part of worship honest. It's the check on religious pride that the whole-life offering requires to stay genuine rather than becoming just another form of performance.

This is what it means to be a stranger in a culture of compromise at the level of the heart. The surrounding culture has no framework for the contrite spirit. It has frameworks for self-improvement, for therapy, for rebranding, for coming back stronger. But the crushed heart that simply comes to God with nothing and trusts His mercy, that's foreign. That's other. That's the kind of poverty the world can't produce and can't replicate. And it's the foundation on which everything else in this chapter, and in this book, has to rest.

Worship as a Life: Recap and What to Do Now

Here's what this chapter has been building toward. Worship isn't an event you attend. It's an existence you inhabit. Your entire bodily life, every task, every relationship, every dollar, every conversation, is the altar on which the offering of your life is placed. That offering begins in brokenness, in the honest acknowledgment of your need for God's mercy, and it extends outward into every corner of your daily existence. The sacred and the secular aren't two different zones.

They're a distinction that Scripture doesn't actually make. There's only life offered to God or life withheld from Him.

A heart that trembles at the Word is the phrase that captures what this looks like internally. Isaiah 66:2 says God looks to the one who is humble and contrite in spirit, and who trembles at His word. Not the one with the most impressive spiritual resume. Not the one who has mastered the theological systems. The one who still comes to Scripture expecting it to say something that requires a response. That posture, humble, expectant, genuinely open to being changed by what God says, is the internal condition that makes whole-life worship possible. Without it, the practices become rituals. With it, even the most ordinary moment becomes an encounter.

The following steps are specific and concrete. They're designed to move you from understanding this to actually living it, starting this week.

First: Identify three daily tasks you'll perform "unto the Lord" starting tomorrow. Don't pick the impressive ones. Pick the ones that feel most ordinary, most invisible, most disconnected from anything spiritual. Maybe it's your commute. Maybe it's a recurring work task you find tedious. Maybe it's a household responsibility you do on autopilot. Pick three specific ones and write them down by name. Then, before you begin each one tomorrow, say this out loud or in your head: "God, I'm offering this to you." That's it. No elaborate prayer. No spiritual performance. Just the deliberate act of lifting the ordinary moment toward God before you do it. Do this for seven consecutive days with the same three tasks. At the end of the seven days, write down one sentence about what changed in how those tasks felt. You're not trying to manufacture a feeling. You're practicing the reorientation of ordinary life toward God. The practice itself is the worship, regardless of what you feel while you're doing it.

Second: Practice a daily prayer of confession for the next two weeks, using this specific structure. Each morning, before you move into the day, spend five minutes with this prayer. Name one specific way you ran your own agenda yesterday rather than God's. Be specific, not general. Not "I was selfish" but "I was impatient with my coworker when they interrupted me because I was more focused on my own productivity than on them as a person." Then say this: "God, I'm bringing this to the altar. I have nothing to offer except what you've given me, and even that I've misused. Have mercy." Then sit in silence for sixty seconds before you move on. The specificity is what makes this work. Vague confession stays in the head. Specific confession reaches the place where the actual idols live. After two weeks of this practice, you'll have a much clearer picture of the recurring patterns where your life keeps crawling off the altar. That clarity is itself a gift. You can't offer what you haven't named.

Third: This week, identify one area of your life where you've been maintaining a performance of spiritual adequacy rather than honest poverty before God. It might be in your prayer life, where you've been going through the motions rather than actually bringing your real questions and fears to God. It might be in a relationship, where you've been presenting a version of yourself that's more spiritually together than you actually are. It might be in your church community, where vulnerability has felt too costly and so you've kept your genuine struggles hidden. Name the area specifically. Then take one concrete step toward honesty in that area this week. Tell one trusted person one true thing about where you actually are spiritually. Bring one real fear to God in prayer instead of the sanitized version you've been praying. Show up to one conversation without the performance. The altar of brokenness isn't built in a single dramatic moment. It's built one honest step at a time. This week's step is the one that matters right now.

Worship as a whole life offered to God is the most defiant thing a believer can do in a culture that has reduced everything, including faith, to a consumer experience. It refuses the Sunday-only container. It refuses the performance of spiritual adequacy. It refuses the false division between sacred tasks and ordinary ones. It says, with every commute and every spreadsheet and every diaper change and every difficult conversation, that all of this belongs to God and all of it is offered to Him. That life looks different. It moves differently. It prioritizes differently. And the people around it eventually notice that they can't quite explain it within the categories the surrounding culture provides. That inexplicability is the witness. Not a program. Not a platform. A life that has genuinely been placed on the altar, crawls back up when it falls off, and keeps returning to the place of honest surrender before a God who does not despise the broken and contrite heart.

10

THE GOD OF MATERIALISM

Jesus talked about money more than almost any other subject. More than heaven. More than hell. More than prayer. That fact alone should stop you. If the Son of God kept returning to this topic, it wasn't because He had a particular interest in personal finance. It was because He could see something about money that most people can't see until it's already done its damage.

He could see that money isn't just money.

In Matthew 6:24, Jesus doesn't say you shouldn't serve God and money. He says you cannot. That single word changes everything. He's not giving you a preference or a strong suggestion. He's describing a structural impossibility built into the human heart. Your heart can only have one ultimate trust. One thing it runs to when things get uncertain. One source it draws its sense of security from. And whatever that thing is, that's what you actually worship, regardless of what you say on Sunday morning.

The ancient word He used was Mammon. That wasn't just slang for cash. In the world Jesus lived in, Mammon carried the weight of a name. A rival. Something that competes for the throne that belongs to God alone. Jesus wasn't saying money is neutral and you just have to be careful with it. He was saying money has a spiritual appetite. It wants your trust. It wants your heart. It wants the place in your life that only God should occupy. And it's extraordinarily good at getting it, because it never announces itself as a god. It announces itself as security, as freedom, as responsibility, as the reasonable thing to pursue.

That's what makes Mammon so dangerous. It doesn't need a temple. It doesn't need a priest. It just needs your anxiety about the future and your desire for control, and it will quietly build an altar in your chest without you ever realizing it happened.

The Mammon Rivalry

The church at Laodicea didn't think they had a problem. That's the most sobering detail in Revelation 3:17. They said, "I am rich, have become wealthy, and have need of nothing." They weren't being arrogant. They were being honest about how things looked from where they were standing. Their material situation was genuinely good. Their community was prosperous. By every visible measure, God had blessed them.

And Jesus told them they were wretched, miserable, poor, blind, and naked.

Not as a metaphor. As a diagnosis. The wealth that made them feel secure had produced a spiritual blindness so complete that they couldn't even see their own condition. They didn't know they were poor. That's the final stage of what Mammon does to a person. It doesn't just make you love money. It makes you so comfortable in your abundance that you lose the capacity to feel your own need for God. The anxiety that would have driven you to prayer has been answered by your savings account. The hunger that would have made you desperate for the Word has been fed by every comfort the world offers. You're full. And fullness, when it comes from the wrong source, is one of the most spiritually dangerous states a person can be in.

Deuteronomy 8:11-18 warned Israel about exactly this before they ever set foot in the Promised Land. God told them that when they'd eaten and were satisfied, when they'd built good houses and their herds had multiplied, when their silver and gold had increased, they would be tempted to say in their hearts, "My power and the might of my hand have gained me this wealth." That's the Laodicean condition in seed form. Prosperity quietly rewrites the story of how you got where you are. God's provision becomes your achievement. His faithfulness becomes your competence. And the moment that rewrite feels natural, Mammon has done its deepest work.

This is also where the prosperity gospel has to be named directly, because it's one of the most significant distortions of Christian faith operating in the church right now. The teaching that God's primary desire for believers is material wealth doesn't just get theology wrong. It gets the direction of the relationship wrong. It turns God into a means to an end, a spiritual mechanism for producing financial outcomes, rather than the end Himself. It takes the very thing Jesus identified as a rival deity and baptizes it in His name. That's not a small error. The Reformers had a phrase for it: golden calf theology. You're using God's name to sanctify exactly what God warned against. The calf is still the calf. The name of the Lord on its side doesn't change what it is.

A person shaped by prosperity gospel thinking doesn't experience Mammon as a rival to God. They experience it as evidence of God's favor. Wealth becomes confirmation that you're right with Him. Poverty becomes evidence that something is spiritually wrong. That framework doesn't just distort your theology. It reshapes your compassion, your generosity, your willingness to take financial risks in obedience to God, and your ability to trust Him when the numbers don't look good. It makes Mammon and God feel like the same thing. And that confusion is more dangerous than outright materialism, because at least outright materialism can be named and repented of.

The rivalry Jesus described in Matthew 6:24 is real and it's active. Mammon competes for the same throne God occupies. Not noisily. Not obviously. But consistently, patiently, and with extraordinary effectiveness. Every financial decision you make is shaped by which of those two you're actually trusting. Not which one you say you trust. Which one your behavior reveals you trust. The ancient writer of Proverbs understood this rivalry and prayed about it with remarkable clarity. "Give me neither poverty nor riches; feed me with the food allotted to me." That prayer isn't timid. It's theologically precise. It's the prayer of someone who understands that both extremes carry spiritual risk, and who trusts God enough to ask for just enough rather than as much as possible.

Breaking the Dissatisfaction Loop

Consumer culture didn't happen by accident. That's worth saying plainly, because most people experience it as simply the world they live in rather than a deliberately constructed system designed to produce a specific result in them. But it is a system. And the result it's designed to produce is dissatisfaction.

Not occasionally. Permanently.

Advertising functions by making you feel that what you have right now is inadequate. That the life you're living is slightly less than it could be. That the gap between where you are and where you want to be can be closed by the next purchase. Every ad you see, every scroll through a curated feed of other people's homes and vacations and clothing and cars, is a small sermon preaching the same gospel: you don't have enough yet. And when you get what you don't have, the sermon starts again about the next thing you're missing. The loop never closes. It was designed not to.

This isn't just a marketing problem. It's a spiritual formation problem. The system is training your heart to look to material things for the satisfaction that only God can provide. Every time you feel the pull of wanting something you don't have, and then feel temporary relief when you get it, followed by the return of the wanting, you're being discipled. Not by a church. By Babylon's economy. And the lesson being taught is that God isn't enough, that His provision isn't sufficient, that the fullness you're looking for is one purchase away.

Think about someone like a hypothetical 34-year-old named Jason, a project manager with a good income, a solid marriage, and a genuine faith. He tithes. He serves at his church. He reads his Bible most mornings. But there's a low-level restlessness that he can't quite shake. He upgraded his phone four months ago and felt great for about a week. He's been looking at kitchen renovations for months. His car is fine, but he's noticed that his neighbor just got a new one and something in him registered it. He doesn't think of himself as materialistic. He thinks of himself as someone who works hard and enjoys the results. But if you tracked his emotional state against his purchasing patterns, you'd find a consistent loop: a vague sense of inadequacy, a specific desire, a purchase, brief satisfaction, and then the return of the vague inadequacy in a slightly different form. He's not a greedy person. He's a person being formed by a system that runs on engineered discontent. And that system is doing its work on him so smoothly that he barely notices it happening.

The biblical concept that breaks this loop isn't deprivation. It's sufficiency. The manna in the wilderness is the clearest picture of it in all of Scripture. God provided exactly what Israel needed for each day. Not more. Not less. Exactly enough. And when they tried to hoard it, it rotted. When they tried to accumulate beyond what the day required, the excess became useless. God was teaching them something through that daily provision that their entire Egyptian formation had worked against: trust Me for today. Don't try to secure tomorrow on your own terms. The manna principle isn't just about food. It's about the posture of a heart that has learned to receive what God gives and trust that it's enough, rather than constantly reaching for more as a hedge against the fear that He might not provide.

Paul understood this posture from the inside. In Philippians 4:11-13, he says something that's easy to read past: "I have learned, in whatever state I am, to be content." Learned. Not received as a gift. Not felt naturally. Learned. Contentment isn't a personality type. It's a discipline. It's something you develop through practice, through choosing to interpret your current situation as sufficient rather than inadequate, through training your desires toward God rather than toward the next thing the system is offering you. Paul wrote those words from prison. His contentment wasn't dependent on his circumstances being comfortable. It was dependent on his trust being correctly placed.

Hebrews 13:5 says it with striking directness: "Let your conduct be without covetousness; be content with such things as you have, for He will never leave nor forsake you." The reason for contentment isn't that you have everything you want. It's that you have the One who will never leave. That's the exchange the manna principle is always pointing toward. Not less stuff. More God. Not the stripping away of comfort as an end in itself. The reorientation of trust toward the One whose presence makes every other form of sufficiency possible.

The dissatisfaction loop breaks when your heart has a different reference point than the one consumer culture is offering. That reference point isn't a budget or a financial philosophy. It's a Person. And the daily practice of returning to that Person, of receiving what He's given as enough, of resisting the system's constant whisper that more is always better, is one of the most countercultural things a believer can do in a world built on the premise that contentment is something you earn by accumulating enough.

Radical Generosity as Separation

Generosity isn't just a nice thing Christians do. It's a declaration of allegiance.

When you give freely, you're doing something to Mammon that nothing else quite accomplishes. You're proving, in the most concrete possible way, that money doesn't have the final claim on your heart. You're demonstrating, with actual dollars, that your security is located somewhere other than your bank account. Every act of genuine generosity is a small act of defiance against the economic logic of Babylon. It says, out loud and in practical terms, that you belong to a different kingdom and operate by different rules.

This is why Jesus connected generosity so directly to the heart. In Matthew 6:21, just a few verses before His statement about not being able to serve both God and Mammon, He said, "Where your treasure is, there your heart will be also." Most people read that as a description of something that's already happened. Where you've already put your money reveals where your heart already is. That's true. But it also works in the other direction. Where you deliberately put your money, your heart will follow. Generosity isn't just the result of a heart that's already free from Mammon. It's one of the primary tools for getting there. You give your way into a freedom that would take years of theological reflection to arrive at any other way.

The early church understood this at a level that made the surrounding culture genuinely confused. Acts 2:44-45 describes believers selling possessions and goods and distributing to anyone who had need. This wasn't a communist economic policy. It was a community whose members had genuinely been freed from the grip of Mammon enough to hold their possessions loosely. They weren't performing generosity. They were living out the logical consequence of actually believing that God provides. If He provides for you, you can give to others. If your security is in Him, you don't need to hoard. The generosity was the visible evidence of a trust that had genuinely been relocated.

That kind of generosity is a form of separation from Babylon's economy in the most practical sense. Babylon's economy runs on accumulation. More is always the goal. Security is always one more layer of financial protection away. The logic of Babylon says you give after you've secured yourself, which means you almost never give enough to feel anything, because the threshold of "enough security" keeps moving. The logic of the kingdom runs in the opposite direction. You give first, from what you have, trusting that God's provision is real. And that giving, done consistently and with genuine sacrifice, produces something in your heart that no amount of financial security can produce. It produces the experience of actually trusting God with something that costs you. And that experience is one of the most powerful antidotes to Mammon's grip that exists.

Proverbs 11:24-25 captures this with a paradox that consumer logic can't process: "There is one who scatters, yet increases more; and there is one who withholds more than is right, but it leads to poverty." The person who gives freely gains. The person who hoards loses. That's not a financial principle. It's a spiritual one. It describes what happens to the heart when it gives versus when it grasps. The grasping heart becomes smaller, more anxious, more calculating, more bound to Mammon. The giving heart becomes larger, freer, more trusting, more genuinely at rest. Generosity doesn't just redistribute money. It redistributes power. Specifically, it takes the power Mammon has claimed over your heart and hands it back to God.

The separation that radical generosity produces is also visible. It's one of the most legible forms of holy defiance available to a believer. In a culture where financial decisions are almost entirely driven by self-interest, where the question behind every major purchase is "what does this do for me?", a person who gives at a level that actually changes their lifestyle is immediately inexplicable. They don't fit the categories. They can't be explained by the surrounding culture's logic. And that inexplicability is exactly what creates the opening for a conversation about the kingdom they actually belong to.

This is what it means to use your resources as a tool for mission rather than a source of security. The money doesn't stop being real. The financial decisions don't stop mattering. But the organizing question behind them shifts from "how do I protect myself?" to "how do I serve others and advance God's purposes?" That shift doesn't happen in a single dramatic moment of consecration. It happens through the repeated, specific, sometimes uncomfortable practice of giving in ways that require you to trust God for what you just gave away.

Spending X-Ray and One Radical Gift

Everything this chapter has covered lands in a practical question: what are you actually going to do differently this week? Understanding Mammon as a rival deity is important. Recognizing the dissatisfaction loop is valuable. But insight that doesn't produce action stays in the head and never reaches the place where Mammon actually lives, which is in your habits, your patterns, and your daily financial decisions.

The following steps are specific. They're designed to move you from awareness to actual reorientation. Work through them in order over the next seven to ten days.

First: Perform a spending X-ray on the last thirty days of your financial life. Pull up your bank statements and credit card history for the past month. Go through every transaction and categorize each one under one of three headings: Need, Desire, or Anxiety. A need is something genuinely required for your life to function. A desire is something you wanted and bought because you wanted it, which isn't automatically wrong. An anxiety purchase is something you bought primarily to manage a feeling, to feel more secure, more adequate, more comfortable, or more in control. Be honest. The anxiety category is where Mammon's work shows up most clearly. After you've categorized everything, look at the pattern. What percentage of your spending is driven by anxiety rather than genuine need or genuine enjoyment of God's good gifts? Write down the two or three specific categories where anxiety-driven spending shows up most consistently. Name them specifically: "I spend here when I feel inadequate about..." or "I buy this when I'm anxious about..." This isn't a guilt exercise. It's a diagnostic. Your spending record is a spiritual X-ray. It shows you where your heart is located, often more accurately than your own self-assessment does. This exercise takes about an hour. Do it before you move to the next step.

Second: Based on what the X-ray revealed, identify one specific Mammon pattern you'll interrupt this week. Not a vague commitment to spend less. One specific pattern. If anxiety about status drives you to upgrade things you don't need, choose one category where you'll deliberately not upgrade for the next ninety days and redirect that money. If boredom or emotional discomfort drives you to online shopping, delete the apps from your phone for thirty days and replace that time with ten minutes of prayer when the urge surfaces. If the dissatisfaction loop is running in a specific area, identify it by name and make one concrete decision that interrupts the loop. Write it down in one sentence: "For the next [specific time period], I will not [specific behavior], and instead I will [specific replacement]." The replacement matters as much as the stopping. You're not just removing a habit. You're relocating the trust that the habit was managing.

Third: Make one radical gift this week. Not a comfortable gift. A gift that requires you to trust God for what you just gave. The amount will be different for everyone. For one person, radical means fifty dollars that they genuinely don't have to spare. For another, it means five hundred. The test isn't the number. The test is whether giving it requires you to actually depend on God's provision rather than your own management. Before you give it, pray this specifically: "God, I'm giving this as a declaration that my security is in you, not in this money. I trust you to provide what I need." Then give it. To a specific person, a specific ministry, or a specific need you're aware of. Not to a category. To something real that you can name. Write down what you gave, to whom, and what it cost you emotionally to give it. That record matters. It's evidence of a transfer of trust that happened in a specific moment. And when Mammon whispers that you were foolish to give it, you'll have something concrete to point to as proof that you chose a different kingdom.

Finally: Pray the Proverbs 30 prayer out loud, once a day for the next two weeks. "Give me neither poverty nor riches; feed me with the food allotted to me." That's it. Pray it in the morning before you check your phone, before you look at your accounts, before the day's financial anxieties have a chance to set the tone. Pray it slowly. Pray it like you mean it. Because what you're doing when you pray it is asking God to be your sufficiency rather than your abundance, which is a very different prayer than most Christians ever pray. You're not asking for more. You're not asking for less. You're asking for exactly what God determines you need, and you're trusting that He knows what that is better than you do. That prayer, prayed consistently over two weeks, does something to your relationship with Mammon that no budget or financial plan can do. It relocates the question of "how much is enough?" from your own calculations to God's provision. And that relocation is the beginning of the freedom this entire chapter has been pointing toward.

The God of materialism is real. Mammon is a genuine rival, not a metaphor, not an abstraction, but a spiritual force that competes for the trust that belongs to God alone. Every believer living in a consumer culture is being formed by that rivalry whether they know it or not. The dissatisfaction loop is running. The anxiety purchases are accumulating. The spiritual blindness that comes from comfortable abundance is settling in quietly, one small compromise at a time.

But the manna still falls. God's provision is still real. The contentment Paul described is still learnable. And the generosity that breaks Mammon's grip is still available to anyone willing to give in a way that actually costs something. Coming out of Egypt's economy doesn't mean becoming poor. It means becoming free. Free from the anxiety that drives accumulation. Free to give without calculating what you'll have left. Free to trust a God whose faithfulness has never once depended on the size of your financial cushion. That freedom is what Babylon's economy can never produce and what the kingdom of God always offers to those who are willing to stop serving two masters and choose the one who actually holds everything.

11

The Idol of Experience

Numbers 11 contains one of the most uncomfortable portraits of God's people in all of Scripture. Israel is in the wilderness. They have manna. Bread from heaven, delivered fresh every morning, the direct and faithful provision of God Himself. And they're weeping. Not because they're starving. Not because God has abandoned them. They're weeping because they miss the food from Egypt. "We remember the fish which we ate freely in Egypt, the cucumbers, the melons, the leeks, the onions, and the garlic."

They had heaven's bread. They wanted Egypt's flavor.

That detail is easy to dismiss as ancient ingratitude until you recognize how precisely it describes the modern Christian's relationship with entertainment, digital stimulation, and the constant demand for new experience. God's provision hasn't changed. His Word is still faithful. His Spirit still moves. Prayer is still the most powerful conversation available to a human being. But compared to the sensory bombardment of streaming services, social media, and a thousand forms of digital content, those things can feel plain. Ordinary. Insufficient. And that feeling, not dramatic apostasy, is the idol this chapter is about.

The Leeks and Garlic of Egypt

The "mixed multitude" that left Egypt with Israel carried something more dangerous than their baggage. They carried their appetites. And those appetites, shaped by four hundred years of Egyptian sensory culture, had no category for manna. Manna was the same every day. It didn't come in different flavors. It didn't compete for attention. It just appeared, quietly, faithfully, every morning, exactly sufficient for the day. And to people whose palates had been formed by the rich, varied, stimulating food culture of Egypt, that faithfulness felt like monotony.

This is a precise portrait of what happens to a soul that has been formed by the entertainment culture of the modern world and then tries to engage with the ordinary means of grace.

God's provision, His Word, prayer, the fellowship of believers, the quiet work of the Spirit in daily life, is faithful. It's nourishing. It's sufficient. But it's often plain. It doesn't arrive with a notification. It doesn't offer a new episode. It doesn't adapt itself to your current mood or optimize itself for your attention span. It just shows up, the same God, the same Word, the same invitation to be still and know. And for a soul that has been trained by years of digital stimulation to expect variety, novelty, and constant sensory engagement, that plainness can feel almost unbearable.

The danger isn't that streaming services or social media are inherently evil. That's an important nuance and it needs to be said clearly. The problem isn't the existence of these things. The problem is what they do to spiritual appetite when consumed without limit. They dull it. Slowly, quietly, without any single moment you could point to as the turning point, the spiritual palate gets recalibrated toward stimulation. And once that recalibration has happened, the bread of God's presence starts to taste like nothing.

Solomon ran this experiment on himself at enormous scale. Ecclesiastes 2:1-11 records his methodical pursuit of every form of pleasure, entertainment, achievement, and sensory experience available to the wealthiest man in the ancient world. He withheld nothing from himself. He gave his heart every joy his eyes desired. And his verdict, delivered with the authority of someone who had actually gone all the way to the bottom of that well, was this: vanity. Grasping for the wind. None of it produced what it promised. The stimulation was real. The satisfaction wasn't.

Isaiah 55:2 asks the same question God has always been asking His people: "Why do you spend money for what is not bread, and your wages for what does not satisfy?" The question isn't rhetorical. It expects an honest answer. And the honest answer for most Christians living in the current moment is that a significant portion of their time, attention, and emotional energy goes toward things that don't satisfy. Not because they're malicious. Because the appetite for stimulation, once formed, keeps demanding to be fed. And the things of God, which actually satisfy at a level nothing else can reach, get crowded out not by a conscious rejection but by a thousand small choices to reach for the leeks instead of the manna.

The experiential expectations this has produced inside the church are worth naming directly. When people arrive at a Sunday gathering having spent the previous week consuming Netflix-quality production, curated social media content, and the best podcasts and music the world has to offer, a simple gathering of believers can feel underwhelming. When sermons are being compared, consciously or not, to TED talks and polished online content, pastors feel pressure to perform rather than simply to preach. When worship is evaluated by the quality of the experience it produces rather than by the faithfulness of the offering being made, the congregation has quietly become consumers rather than worshippers. The idol of experience doesn't require anyone to consciously abandon God. It just requires that God's provision be held up against Egypt's flavors and found wanting.

Moses rejected every one of Pharaoh's compromises, as we saw in Chapter 1. But this particular compromise, the one that says you can worship God while keeping Egypt's appetites fully intact, is the one that's hardest to see because it doesn't feel like a compromise. It feels like preference. It feels like personality. It feels like simply being a person of your time. And that invisibility is exactly what makes it so effective at holding people in Egypt while they believe they've already left.

Hebrews 11:24-26 describes Moses making a choice that cuts directly against this. He chose to suffer with God's people rather than enjoy the fleeting pleasures of Egypt's court. The pleasures of Egypt were real. The text doesn't pretend otherwise. Moses genuinely had access to something the wilderness couldn't offer in terms of sensory comfort and cultural richness. He chose the reproach of Christ instead, because he was looking toward a reward that Egypt's pleasures could never produce. That's not asceticism for its own sake. That's a person who had correctly evaluated what each option actually delivers and chosen accordingly.

The invitation of this chapter is the same invitation. Not to pretend that Egypt's flavors aren't real or that the stimulation isn't genuinely pleasurable. But to ask honestly what it's costing you. What has the constant diet of digital stimulation done to your capacity for silence? What has the demand for new experience done to your ability to receive the faithful, plain, daily bread that God keeps offering? Those questions deserve honest answers. Because the distance between where most Christians currently are and where God is inviting them isn't primarily a moral distance. It's an appetite problem. And appetite problems require a different kind of solution than willpower alone can provide.

The Rewired Brain

T.S. Eliot described the modern condition as being "distracted from distraction by distraction." He wrote that in the mid-twentieth century, before smartphones existed, before social media, before the algorithm. He was describing something he could already see in the cultural trajectory of his time. If he were writing today, he'd need stronger language.

The contemporary experience is one of perpetual stimulation. There is no longer a default state of quiet. Every waiting room has a screen. Every car ride has a podcast. Every moment of potential silence has a phone to fill it. The never-ending scroll is always available, the constant feed always refreshing, the always-available library of content always offering something new. And the result isn't just wasted time. The result is a rewired brain.

Neuroscience has been documenting this for years. Constant stimulation shortens attention spans. It impairs the capacity for deep thinking. It reduces the ability to sustain focus on a single thing for an extended period without the pull toward something new becoming almost physically uncomfortable. These aren't minor inconveniences. They're structural changes to how the brain processes information and manages attention. And the spiritual implications of those changes are more serious than most Christians have stopped to consider.

Psalm 46:10 says, "Be still, and know that I am God." That verse has been quoted so often it's become almost decorative. But read it as a prescription for a specific spiritual problem and it becomes urgent. Stillness is the condition God names for a particular kind of knowing. Not information about God. Knowing God. The kind of encounter that changes you rather than merely informing you. And that encounter requires something the digital world is systematically dismantling: the capacity to be still.

If you've lost the ability to be still, you've lost the capacity for the kind of encounter God is offering in silence. That's not an exaggeration. It's a direct consequence. Prayer that goes deep requires sustained attention. Meditation on Scripture requires the ability to sit with a single passage long enough for it to reach below the surface of the mind. Hearing the still, small voice that spoke to Elijah in 1 Kings 19 requires a quality of inner quiet that Egypt's noise makes impossible. The prophet didn't encounter God in the wind, the earthquake, or the fire. He encountered Him in the sound of a gentle blowing. A soul that has been trained to need constant stimulation will never hear that sound. Not because God isn't speaking. Because the noise is too loud and the capacity for quiet has atrophied.

Think about what this looks like in a real person's life. Consider a hypothetical 38-year-old named Daniel, a committed Christian who leads a small group at his church, reads theology, and genuinely wants to grow in his faith. He has a Bible app, a prayer app, and three Christian podcasts he rotates through on his commute. He listens to worship music while he works. He follows several pastors and theologians on social media. By any external measure, he's consuming more Christian content than at any point in his life. But his actual prayer life, the kind where he sits in silence before God without anything playing, has essentially collapsed. He can't sustain it for more than three minutes before the pull toward his phone becomes overwhelming. He's consuming more about God than ever and encountering God less than ever. The content has become a substitute for the encounter. And the irony is that even his spiritual consumption has become a form of the same stimulation problem it was supposed to address.

This pattern matters because it's not primarily a discipline failure. It's a formation problem. Daniel doesn't lack willpower in other areas of his life. He's disciplined at work. He exercises consistently. But his attention has been so thoroughly shaped by a high-stimulation environment that the specific kind of sustained, quiet, receptive attention that prayer and Scripture meditation require has become genuinely difficult. The muscle has atrophied. And atrophied muscles don't recover through guilt. They recover through gradual, consistent, patient exercise.

The connection between this and the book's central call is direct. Living as a stranger in a culture of compromise means refusing to let the culture define what your inner life looks like. And the culture is currently defining the inner lives of most Christians by default, through the habits it has formed in them before they thought to resist. A soul that cannot be still cannot fully receive what God offers in silence. A mind that has been rewired for constant novelty will find the unchanging faithfulness of God's Word hard to appreciate. A heart that has been trained to locate spiritual experience in emotional peaks will struggle to recognize God in the quiet, ordinary, daily faithfulness of His presence. Recovering the inner life isn't optional for the person who wants to live as a genuine stranger in this culture. It's the prerequisite for everything else.

The recovery begins with an honest assessment of where things actually are. Not where you wish they were. Not where they used to be. Where they are right now. How long can you sit in complete silence before the discomfort becomes overwhelming? How many consecutive minutes can you read Scripture without reaching for your phone? When did you last spend fifteen uninterrupted minutes in prayer with no music, no app, no structure, just you and God? Those questions aren't meant to produce shame. They're meant to produce an accurate starting point. You can't recover something you haven't honestly diagnosed as lost.

The good news is that what has been formed can be reformed. The brain that has been shaped by constant stimulation can be reshaped by consistent practice of stillness. The appetite that has been calibrated toward novelty can be recalibrated toward the faithful and the plain. But it doesn't happen by accident, and it doesn't happen quickly. It happens through the deliberate, repeated, sometimes uncomfortable choice to create space for silence and to stay in that space long enough for something to grow there. That's the work this section is pointing toward, and the next two sections will show you specifically how to do it.

Cultivating a Taste for God

There's a difference between entertainment and recreation that most people have never stopped to name. The distinction matters more than it might initially seem, because collapsing the two leaves you without the ability to tell which one you're actually doing at any given moment.

Entertainment fills time. It occupies attention. It produces a pleasant experience while it's happening and leaves you roughly where you were when it started. There's nothing necessarily wrong with it. But it doesn't restore anything. It doesn't replenish. It doesn't send you back into your life with more capacity than you had before. It's neutral at best, and at the volumes most people consume it, it becomes actively draining.

Recreation, in its original sense, means re-creation. It restores. It sends you back into your life with something renewed, whether that's physical energy, emotional equilibrium, creative capacity, or spiritual attentiveness. A long walk in nature can be recreation. A genuine conversation with a trusted friend can be recreation. Reading a novel that expands your imagination and your empathy can be recreation. Sabbath rest, practiced as God designed it, is the deepest form of recreation available. The question that distinguishes entertainment from recreation isn't what the activity looks like from the outside. It's what it produces on the inside.

A simple diagnostic question cuts through the confusion every time: does this activity leave me more or less hungry for God? More or less present to the people around me? More or less able to hear the still, small voice? Those three questions applied honestly to any activity will tell you whether it's filling time or restoring your soul. They don't require a theology degree. They just require the honesty to answer them accurately rather than defensively.

Psalm 16:11 says, "In Your presence is fullness of joy; at Your right hand are pleasures forevermore." That verse isn't describing a feeling you produce by trying hard enough to feel spiritual. It's describing a reality that becomes accessible when you've cultivated the capacity to receive it. Fullness of joy. Not the temporary relief that entertainment provides. Not the brief satisfaction of a new experience. Fullness. The kind that doesn't leave a gap that immediately needs to be filled again. But that fullness requires a cultivated taste. It requires a willingness to be weaned from sugar in order to appreciate bread.

That's not a comfortable process. Anyone who has ever tried to significantly reduce sugar in their actual diet knows that the first week is genuinely unpleasant. The things that used to taste sweet start to taste bland. The things that were always there but were being drowned out by sweetness start to become detectable. And eventually, after enough time has passed, your palate recalibrates. Fruit that would have tasted boring before starts to taste genuinely sweet. The flavors that were always present but inaccessible become available. The recalibration is real. But it requires a period of discomfort that most people aren't willing to sit through.

The spiritual parallel is exact. The person who reduces their consumption of constant digital stimulation will almost certainly find the first week uncomfortable. The silence will feel heavy. The Bible will feel flat. Prayer will feel like talking to a wall. That's not evidence that God has withdrawn. That's evidence that the recalibration is beginning. The spiritual palate is adjusting. The noise that was drowning out the still, small voice is starting to subside. And if you stay in that discomfort long enough, something begins to shift. The Word starts to carry weight it didn't carry before. Prayer starts to feel less like a performance and more like an actual conversation. The presence of God, which was always there, starts to become perceptible in ways that the noise had made impossible.

Paul's testimony in Philippians 4:11-13 describes this as something he learned rather than something he received automatically. "I have learned, in whatever state I am, to be content." The contentment Paul describes isn't just financial. It's existential. It's the settled sufficiency of a person who has discovered that Christ is genuinely enough, not as a theological statement but as a lived experience. That kind of contentment doesn't come from having enough stimulation. It comes from having enough of God. And having enough of God requires the willingness to stop filling every available space with something else.

Colossians 3:1-3 gives the theological foundation for this reorientation. "If you were raised with Christ, seek those things which are above, where Christ is, sitting at the right hand of God. Set your mind on things above, not on things on the earth." Set your mind. That's an active verb. It describes a deliberate act of will, a choice made repeatedly, a direction of attention that has to be chosen against the pull of everything competing for it. The person who has set their mind on things above isn't someone who has stopped caring about the world they live in. They're someone who has established a reference point that gives everything else its proper proportion. And from that reference point, the leeks and garlic of Egypt start to look like exactly what they are: not ultimate satisfaction, but a poor substitute for something infinitely better.

The practical work of cultivating a taste for God isn't complicated. But it does require specificity, because vague intentions to "spend more time with God" don't survive contact with the actual demands of daily life. What survives is specific practice, scheduled and protected, repeated consistently enough to begin forming new habits of attention.

A generation addicted to excitement must rediscover the joy of quiet faithfulness. That rediscovery doesn't happen through a conference or a powerful worship experience or a new devotional plan. It happens through the unglamorous, daily, repeated choice to sit in silence before God and stay there even when nothing dramatic is happening. The manna doesn't look impressive. It never did. But it's what sustained Israel in the wilderness. And the quiet, faithful, daily presence of God is what sustains the believer who has learned to receive it rather than constantly reaching past it toward something more stimulating.

Recap and What to Do Now

This chapter has traced a single thread from Israel's craving in the wilderness to the screen in your pocket. The thread is this: when appetite gets formed by constant stimulation, the faithful provision of God starts to feel insufficient. Not because it is insufficient, but because the palate has been recalibrated away from it. The idol of experience doesn't require you to consciously reject God. It just requires that you keep reaching for Egypt's flavors until God's bread no longer registers as food.

The path back isn't complicated. But it is specific. The following steps are designed to be done in order, starting this week. They're not suggestions for someday. They're moves you can make right now that will begin the recalibration.

First: Do a 24-hour digital fast, starting tomorrow. Not a vague reduction in screen time. A complete fast. From the moment you wake up until the same time the following day, no social media, no streaming, no news, no podcasts, no scrolling of any kind. Your phone can be used for calls and necessary messages. Nothing else. Before you begin, write down this question on a piece of paper: "What surfaces when the noise stops?" Keep that paper with you for the 24 hours. Every time you feel the pull toward your phone, write down what you were feeling in that moment. Not a long journal entry. One word or one sentence. Boredom? Anxiety? Loneliness? Habit? The discomfort you feel is information. It's showing you what the stimulation has been managing in you that you haven't been bringing to God. At the end of the 24 hours, read back through what you wrote. That list is a map of the places where Egypt's flavors have been doing the work that God's presence is supposed to do.

Second: Spend 15 minutes in complete silence each day for the next two weeks. Not 15 minutes of worship music. Not 15 minutes of a devotional app. Silence. Set a timer for 15 minutes. Sit in a chair with no phone, no music, no background noise. Open your Bible to one passage, something short, a single psalm or a few verses from the

Gospels. Read it once, slowly. Then put it down and sit with what you read for the rest of the time. Don't try to generate thoughts or feelings. Don't evaluate whether the time is going well. Just stay. If your mind wanders, gently return to the passage. Do this at the same time each day, in the same place if possible. The consistency of location and time matters because you're building a new habit of attention, and habits form through repetition in consistent contexts. By the end of two weeks, write down one honest sentence about what changed. Not what you think should have changed. What actually did.

Third: Apply the three-question diagnostic to your current entertainment habits this week. Pick the three forms of entertainment or digital content you consume most regularly. For each one, answer these three questions in writing. Does this leave me more or less hungry for God? More or less present to the people around me? More or less able to hear the still, small voice? Be specific in your answers. Don't answer in the abstract. Answer based on what you actually notice in yourself after consuming this content. If a habit fails all three questions, cut it for thirty days. Not forever. Thirty days. If it fails two of three, reduce it significantly and replace the time with something from the recreation category, something that actually restores rather than just occupies. Write down the specific change you're making and the specific replacement. Vague intentions don't produce actual change. A sentence that reads "I will stop watching [specific thing] after 9pm and spend that time reading [specific book]" is a plan. Everything else is a wish.

Finally: Choose one form of recreation this week that you've been neglecting in favor of entertainment. Something that genuinely restores you. A long walk without headphones. An hour of reading a book that expands your imagination. A real conversation with someone you love, phones away, full attention given. Time in a garden, a workshop, a kitchen, doing something with your hands that produces something tangible. Whatever it is for you, schedule it specifically. Put it in your calendar as a protected appointment. Then, before you begin it, say this: "God, I'm receiving this as a gift from you. I'm asking you to meet me in it." That simple act of intentionality changes the category of the activity. It moves it from time-filling to soul-restoring. And over time, that shift in how you receive the ordinary good things of life is part of what it means to cultivate a taste for God rather than a taste for Egypt.

The fullness of joy that Psalm 16:11 describes is real. It's available. It's not reserved for monks or mystics or people with unusually quiet lives. It's available to a 38-year-old school teacher, a marketing manager, a pastor, a parent of young children, anyone who is willing to do the unglamorous work of recalibrating their appetite away from constant stimulation and toward the faithful, plain, nourishing presence of a God who has been offering Himself all along. The leeks and garlic of Egypt were never going to satisfy. They never do. The manna has always been there. Learning to taste it again is one of the most defiant things you can do in a culture that has made constant stimulation feel like a right.

12

— · —

THE WILDERNESS OF TRANSFORMATION

Nobody volunteers for the wilderness.

You don't wake up one morning and think, "I'd really love to have everything stripped away, my routines disrupted, my comfortable props removed, and my deepest assumptions about God tested until I don't know what I'm standing on anymore." Nobody signs up for that. But God keeps leading His people there anyway. Not because He's cruel. Not because He's forgotten them. Because the wilderness is the only classroom that teaches certain things, and those things can't be learned anywhere else.

Deuteronomy 8:2-3 is one of the most clarifying verses in all of Scripture for understanding why hard seasons happen. God told Israel to remember that He led them through forty years in the wilderness "to humble you and test you, to know what was in your heart, whether you would keep His commandments or not." Three things stand out in that sentence and they're worth sitting with carefully. God led them, meaning the wilderness wasn't an accident or a mistake or a sign that something had gone wrong. God tested them, meaning the purpose was diagnostic and formative, not random. And God wanted to know what was in their hearts, meaning the wilderness exposes what prosperity conceals. You don't know what you really trust until the things you've been trusting are taken away.

That last piece is the one most people miss. Prosperity hides things. When everything is going well, when the income is steady and the relationships are stable and the health is good and the routine is comfortable, you can't fully see what your heart is actually running on. You think you're trusting God. You might genuinely be trusting God, at least partially. But you can't know how deep that trust goes until the other options are removed. The wilderness removes the other options. And what's left after the removal is the honest answer to the question God was always asking.

God's Chosen Classroom

The wilderness has a reputation problem. When most Christians hear the word, they associate it with failure, punishment, or spiritual drought. Something went wrong. God is displeased. The enemy is attacking. The wilderness must mean something bad is happening, and the goal is to get out of it as fast as possible.

But that's not what Scripture says about it. Not even close.

Look at the pattern across the biblical story. Moses encountered the living God at a burning bush in the wilderness of Midian, Exodus 3. That wilderness moment didn't end his story. It launched it. Elijah, after one of the greatest prophetic victories in Israel's history on Mount Carmel, fled into the wilderness of Sinai in fear and exhaustion. He sat under a broom tree and asked God to let him die. And God didn't rebuke him. God fed him, twice, and then met him on the mountain in a still, small voice that Elijah had never heard before. The fire and the wind and the earthquake passed, and God was in none of them. He was in the quiet. But Elijah could only hear that quiet because everything else had been stripped away. David wrote some of his most intimate psalms from the Judean wilderness, hunted and hiding and utterly dependent. John the Baptist prepared the way of the Lord from the wilderness, not from a palace or a temple court. And Jesus Himself, before His public ministry began, was led by the Spirit into the wilderness for forty days.

Led by the Spirit. Into the wilderness.

That detail in Matthew 4:1 is worth stopping on. Jesus didn't stumble into the wilderness. He wasn't driven there by failure or sin or the enemy's schemes. The Holy Spirit led Him there deliberately. The same Spirit who descended on Him at His baptism like a dove immediately drove Him into a place of deprivation and testing. This was the plan. The wilderness wasn't a detour from Jesus' mission. It was the preparation for it. The forty days of hunger and temptation and isolation weren't something to be survived before the real work started. They were part of the real work. They were where Jesus demonstrated, in the most stripped-down conditions possible, that His dependence on the Father was total and unshakeable.

The temptations Jesus faced in the wilderness are worth looking at closely, because they're not random. Each one was a specific invitation to short-circuit dependence on God. Turn these stones into bread. Prove your identity by forcing God's hand. Take the kingdoms of the world through a different path than the cross. Every temptation was essentially the same offer: use your own power, take the shortcut, stop depending on the Father's provision and timing. And Jesus refused every single one. Not through gritted-teeth willpower. Through the Word of God, spoken with the calm authority of someone who had genuinely settled the question of where His dependence lay. "Man shall not live by bread alone, but by every word that proceeds from the mouth of God." That's not a theological statement made from comfort. That's a declaration made from hunger. And hunger is the wilderness's most effective teacher.

The manna narrative in Exodus 16 teaches the same lesson through a different angle. God provided bread from heaven for Israel in the wilderness, but He designed it with specific limitations. You couldn't stockpile it. Exodus 16:19-20 records the instruction clearly: don't leave any until morning. The people who tried to save some overnight found it bred worms and stank. The provision was daily, deliberate, and non-negotiable in its terms. You couldn't manage your way around the dependence. You couldn't be clever enough or organized enough to get ahead of the need. Every single morning, you needed God to do it again. And every single morning, He did.

The manna taught four things simultaneously. It taught dependence, because you couldn't stockpile it. It taught humility, because it wasn't what anyone would have chosen. It taught obedience, because the gathering rules had to be followed exactly. And it taught trust, because it appeared faithfully every morning without fail. These four lessons don't come from a textbook. They come from forty years of waking up with nothing and watching God provide. That's the wilderness classroom. You can't learn what the manna teaches while you still have Egypt's storehouses to fall back on.

James 1:2-4 frames this with a counterintuitive logic that's easy to read past. "Count it all joy when you fall into various trials, knowing that the testing of your faith produces patience." Count it joy. Not pretend it's fine. Not perform happiness about it. Actually count it, calculate it, assess it as something worth rejoicing in. Because the testing of your faith produces something. It produces patience, which in the Greek carries the idea of steadfast endurance under pressure. The kind of character that doesn't collapse when things get hard. The kind of faith that has been tested enough to know it holds. You don't get that from comfortable seasons. You get it from the wilderness.

Romans 5:3-5 extends the chain further. Tribulation produces perseverance. Perseverance produces character. Character produces hope. And this hope doesn't disappoint, because the love of God has been poured into our hearts by the Holy Spirit. That's a specific sequence, and it starts in a place no one would choose voluntarily. The hope that doesn't disappoint isn't the hope of someone who has never had their hopes tested. It's the hope of someone who has been through the tribulation and come out the other side with a character that was built in the fire. The wilderness is where that chain begins.

First Peter 1:6-7 uses the image of gold refined by fire. Your faith, Peter says, is more precious than gold that perishes. And gold doesn't get refined by being kept comfortable. It gets refined by heat, by the process that burns away everything that isn't gold and leaves only what's pure. The wilderness is that refining process. The scarcity, the waiting, the uncertainty, the stripping away of the props you've been leaning on, all of it is the fire that reveals what your faith is actually made of. Not to condemn you. To purify you. To remove what isn't genuine and leave what is.

John 15:1-8 adds one more image. Jesus describes the Father as a vinedresser who prunes the branches that bear fruit so they'll bear more fruit. Pruning isn't punishment. It's precision. The vinedresser isn't cutting the branch because it's bad. He's cutting it because he can see what it could become with less of the wrong things competing for its energy. Wilderness seasons are often God's pruning shears. Not removing what's fruitful. Removing what's hindering deeper fruitfulness. What gets cut away in the wilderness, the false securities, the misplaced trusts, the comfortable substitutes for genuine dependence, those things weren't bearing fruit anyway. And their removal makes room for something that will.

There's a common misconception that needs to be addressed directly here, because it causes enormous damage to people who are already in a hard season. The misconception is that suffering always means either God's displeasure or the enemy's attack. If things are hard, either you've done something wrong and God is punishing you, or the devil is after you. Those two options exhaust most people's framework for interpreting difficulty. But sometimes it's neither. Sometimes the hard season is the deliberate, loving work of a God who is forming Christ in His people, who is doing exactly what Deuteronomy 8:2 describes, leading His people through a wilderness to humble them and test them and know what's in their hearts. The wilderness isn't punishment. It's formation. And the difference between those two interpretations changes everything about how you respond to it.

Consider someone like a hypothetical 41-year-old named Sarah, a worship leader and mother of three who has been in ministry for fifteen years. Two years ago, her church went through a painful split. Her income dropped significantly. Her closest friendships fractured. A health issue surfaced that required months of treatment. From the outside, it looked like everything was falling apart at once. And for the first several months, Sarah interpreted all of it through the lens of spiritual attack or divine displeasure. She kept asking what she'd done wrong. She kept looking for the sin that had caused the collapse. But as she sat with Deuteronomy 8 and let it actually land, something shifted. She began to see that God was exposing things the busy, successful years of ministry had concealed. He was showing her how much of her sense of identity had been built on her role rather than on who He said she was. He was revealing that several of her closest relationships had been built on shared ministry performance rather than genuine covenant love. He was stripping away the props, not to destroy her, but to show her what was underneath them. The wilderness wasn't the enemy of her faith. It was doing things to her faith that the fruitful years never could have done.

That reframe doesn't make the wilderness painless. It makes it purposeful. And purposeful pain is something a person can endure in a way that random, meaningless suffering simply isn't. When you know that God led you here, that the testing is diagnostic and formative, that He's after your heart and not your destruction, the wilderness becomes something you can cooperate with rather than just survive. That cooperation is what this chapter is calling you toward.

The Allure of the Desert

Hosea 2:14-15 contains one of the most surprising images in all of Scripture for anyone who has been thinking about the wilderness as primarily a place of hardship. God says to His people, "I will allure her, will bring her into the wilderness, and speak comfort to her." That word "allure" is the key. In the Hebrew, it carries the idea of gentle seduction, of drawing someone toward you with tenderness and intimacy. It's not the language of a judge sentencing a criminal. It's the language of a bridegroom drawing his bride away from the noise and the crowd so he can have her to himself.

God allures His people into the wilderness.

That reframes everything. The desert isn't where God sends you when He's finished with you. It's where He takes you when He wants you most fully. It's where He removes the competitors, the noise, the distractions, the props, everything that has been filling the space between you and Him, so that He can speak directly, tenderly, intimately, in a way that the crowded life makes almost impossible. The wilderness, in Hosea's image, is where the bridegroom speaks comfort to the bride. It's the most intimate space in the relationship, not the most abandoned one.

This is the thing that Egypt can never offer. Egypt is full. Full of stimulation, full of provision, full of structure and routine and the comfortable hum of a life that doesn't require God for its daily operation. Egypt has everything you need to get through the day without praying. The wilderness has nothing except God. And that's precisely the point. When God is the only option, you discover whether He's actually enough. And the people who have made that discovery, who have been through the wilderness and come out the other side knowing from the inside that God is sufficient, carry something the people of Egypt can't manufacture. They carry a settled trust that doesn't depend on circumstances being favorable. They know the manna falls. They've seen it with their own eyes.

Elijah's encounter at Horeb in 1 Kings 19 is one of the most tender wilderness moments in Scripture. He'd just come off the greatest prophetic victory of his life on Mount Carmel. Fire had fallen. The prophets of Baal had been defeated. The people had fallen on their faces and declared, "The Lord, He is God." And then one threatening message from Jezebel sent him running into the wilderness, so depleted and desperate that he sat under a broom tree and asked God to take his life. He was done.

God's response to that brokenness is worth reading slowly. He didn't rebuke Elijah. He didn't question his faith or his courage. He sent an angel who touched him and said, "Arise and eat." There was bread and water waiting. He ate. He slept. The angel came again. "Arise and eat, because the journey is too great for you." God fed him twice before He said a single word about the mission or the future. The wilderness first produced the stripping, and then it produced the care. And then, at the mountain, it produced the encounter. Not in the wind or the earthquake or the fire. In the still, small voice. The sound of a gentle blowing. The kind of voice you can only hear when everything else has gone quiet.

That's what the wilderness is for. It quiets everything that has been drowning out the gentle voice. The props of life, the busyness, the noise, the comfortable routines, the financial cushions, the social structures, all of them are forms of sound. Not evil sound, necessarily. Just sound. And when God allures you into the wilderness and removes them one by one, what's left is the silence that makes His voice finally audible. The people who have heard that voice, who have encountered God in the stripped-down quiet of a season where everything else was gone, don't go back to Egypt willingly. They've tasted something there that Egypt never offered and can never replicate.

The broader pattern of Scripture reinforces this. The wilderness is where God meets His people at pivotal moments, not at the edges of those moments but at the center of them. Moses didn't receive his calling in Pharaoh's palace. He received it in the wilderness, at a burning bush that wasn't consumed. The burning bush itself is an image of what the wilderness does. The fire burns but doesn't destroy. The presence of God is intense but not consuming. The encounter is transformative without being obliterating. That's the wilderness encounter. It changes you without destroying you. It burns away what isn't real without touching what is.

The concept of the props being removed deserves more attention, because it's one of the most practically important things about wilderness seasons. A prop is anything that provides what only God should provide. Financial security can be a prop when it's doing the work of trust. A relationship can be a prop when it's doing the work of identity. A ministry role can be a prop when it's doing the work of significance.

Busyness can be a prop when it's doing the work of worth. None of these things are inherently wrong. But when they're functioning as load-bearing walls in your soul, bearing weight that belongs to God alone, they've become props. And God, in His mercy, removes the props. Not to leave you without support. To become the support. To show you that He can hold what the props were holding, and hold it better, and hold it without the conditions and limitations and fragility that every human prop eventually reveals.

The person who has never had their props removed doesn't know this from experience. They believe it theologically, perhaps. They can quote the verses. But there's a difference between believing that God is sufficient and knowing it from the inside, from having been in the place where He was the only option and discovering that He showed up. The wilderness produces that knowledge. And that knowledge, once you have it, changes the entire texture of your faith. You stop white-knuckling your security. You stop managing your life with the anxious grip of someone who knows everything will fall apart if they let go. You hold things more loosely because you've discovered that the One who is truly holding you doesn't let go.

The allure of the desert, in the end, is the allure of genuine intimacy with God. Not the managed, surface-level relationship that a comfortable life makes possible. The kind that's forged in the place where there's nothing else to hold onto. The kind that Hosea describes as a bridegroom speaking comfort to a bride he's drawn away from the noise specifically so she can hear him. That intimacy is the wilderness's deepest gift. And it can't be received any other way.

Living as a stranger in a culture of compromise means being willing to go where God leads, even when He leads somewhere uncomfortable. The culture of compromise offers a faith that never has to leave Egypt, a faith that stays comfortable and manageable and never costs anything significant. But the holy defiance this book has been calling you toward is a different kind of faith altogether. It's the faith of people who have been allured into the wilderness and discovered there that God is exactly who He said He was. That faith doesn't need the culture's approval. It doesn't need the props that Egypt provides. It has something better. It has the still, small voice. And once you've heard it in the silence, the noise of Egypt stops being quite so compelling.

Recap and What to Do Now

This chapter has covered two interconnected realities about the wilderness. First, that God leads His people into it deliberately, as a diagnostic and formative space where the heart gets tested and the deep work of transformation happens. Second, that God allures His people into it intimately, drawing them away from the noise and the props so He can speak comfort and build the kind of trust that only forms when He's the only option left.

The wilderness isn't the opposite of God's presence. It's often the place of His most concentrated presence. The stripping away of props isn't punishment. It's preparation. The testing isn't rejection. It's refinement. And the alluring into the desert isn't abandonment. It's the most intimate invitation God offers.

The following steps are specific and designed to move you from understanding this to actively cooperating with what God may already be doing in a current wilderness season.

First: Identify the current wilderness in your life and name it specifically on paper. Don't use vague language. Don't write "things are hard." Write the actual thing. "I've been in a season of financial scarcity for eight months and I don't know when it will change." "My marriage has been in a painful place for two years." "My health situation has removed my ability to do the things that used to give me a sense of purpose." "My ministry role ended and I don't know who I am without it." Whatever it is, name it in one or two specific sentences. Then write this question beside it: "God, what are you exposing in me through this?" Not "what are you doing to me?" but "what are you exposing in me?" The difference in those two questions is significant. The first positions you as a passive recipient of God's actions. The second positions you as someone actively trying to cooperate with what God is doing. Sit with that question for ten minutes in silence. Write down whatever surfaces, even if it's partial, even if it's uncomfortable. You don't have to have the full answer. You just have to be willing to ask the question honestly.

Second: Identify one prop that the current wilderness has removed or is removing, and write a specific prayer of release about it. A prop is something that has been providing what only God should provide. Go back to the categories from earlier in this chapter: financial security, a relationship, a ministry role, busyness, a sense of control over outcomes. Pick the one that the current season has most clearly disrupted. Then write a prayer, by hand, in your journal or on a piece of paper, that follows this specific structure. Name the prop by its exact function: "God, I've been getting my sense of [security, identity, significance, worth] from [specific thing]." Then acknowledge what the removal has revealed: "The loss of this has shown me that I was trusting it more than I was trusting you." Then make the transfer explicit: "I'm asking you to be my [security, identity, significance, worth] in a way that this thing never actually could be." Keep that prayer somewhere you can read it again when the wilderness gets hard. It's not a magic formula. It's a record of a specific moment of reorientation that you can return to when you need to remember what you decided in the quiet.

Third: Create one specific daily practice for the next thirty days that protects space for the still, small voice. The wilderness does its deepest work in silence, and silence requires protection in a world that fills every available space with noise. Choose a specific time, a specific length, and a specific location. The time should be the same every day. The length should be at least fifteen minutes. The location should be somewhere you can sit without interruption. During that time, no phone, no music, no devotional app. Open your Bible to a single short passage, read it once slowly, then put it down and sit in silence with what you read. You're not trying to generate insights or feelings. You're creating the conditions for the still, small voice to be heard. At the end of each week, write one sentence about what you noticed during those times. Not what you think you should have noticed. What you actually noticed. After thirty days, you'll have a record of what God was saying in the silence. That record is worth more than you can anticipate right now.

Finally: Write a one-paragraph declaration about your current wilderness season that reflects the Deuteronomy 8 framing rather than the punishment framing. This is the interpretive work that changes everything. Instead of "I don't know why this is happening to me," write something that reflects what you've learned in this chapter. It might sound like this: "God led me into this season deliberately. He's testing what's in my heart. He's exposing where my trust was misplaced. He's removing props so He can become the foundation they were pretending to be. He's alluring me into a place of deeper intimacy where the noise of my comfortable life couldn't reach. This season isn't a sign that He's abandoned me. It's a sign that He's after something in me that the comfortable seasons couldn't produce." Write your own version of that in your own words. Make it specific to your actual situation. Then read it out loud once a day for the next two weeks, specifically on the days when the wilderness feels most like punishment. You're not pretending the pain isn't real. You're choosing the interpretation that's actually true, the one that God Himself gave in Deuteronomy 8, and training your mind to hold it even when your circumstances argue for a different story.

The wilderness has always been where God does His most intimate and transformative work. From Moses at the burning bush to Elijah in the silence to Jesus in the forty days to every believer who has ever been led somewhere stripped and quiet and discovered God there, the pattern holds. He led them. He tested them. He spoke comfort to them. He became their provision. And they came out the other side knowing something about His faithfulness that no comfortable season could have taught them. That knowledge is what makes a person genuinely different from the culture around them. Not a different set of opinions. Not a different political identity. A different foundation. The kind that has been tested by fire and found to hold.

13

— · —

RETURNING TO THE MISSION

Every chapter in this book has been moving toward a single question. Not "how do I protect myself from the world?" but "what am I being made holy for?" Those are very different questions. The first one builds walls. The second one opens doors. And the answer Scripture gives to that second question is the same answer it has given in every generation since Abraham packed up his tent in Ur and started walking toward a land he couldn't see.

You were called out in order to be sent back in.

That's the pivot this chapter makes. Everything that came before, the naming of idols, the wilderness stripping, the reorientation of worship, the recovery of genuine dependence on God, all of it was preparation. Not an end in itself. Preparation for something God has always had in mind for the people He calls out of the world's system. He doesn't call them out so they can build a comfortable compound away from everything messy and compromised. He calls them out so that what gets formed in them through separation can be carried back into the very spaces they came from, as a witness to something the world can't produce on its own.

Sanctified for Sending

John 17 is where Jesus prays the night before His crucifixion, and the prayer He prays for His disciples is one of the most carefully structured statements about mission in the entire New Testament. He doesn't ask the Father to remove His followers from the world. He's very specific about that. "I do not pray that You should take them out of the world, but that You should keep them from the evil one." And then He says something that changes the entire frame: "Sanctify them by Your truth. As You sent Me into the world, I also have sent them into the world."

The order in that prayer matters enormously. Sanctification comes before sending. You aren't sent out to become holy somewhere along the way. You're made holy so that you can be sent effectively. The wilderness, the stripping, the reorientation of trust, the recovery of genuine worship, all of that is the sanctification that precedes the sending. God doesn't skip that step. He never has.

Look at the pattern across the biblical story and it becomes impossible to miss. God called Abraham out of Ur, and the purpose of that departure was stated plainly in Genesis 12:3: "In you all the families of the earth shall be blessed." Abraham wasn't called out so he could build a separate, protected community of people who avoided contact with the surrounding nations. He was called out so that through him something would reach every family on earth. The separation was real. The mission was global. Both were true at the same time, and neither could function without the other.

Israel's story carries the same structure. Isaiah 49:6 records God saying, "It is too small a thing that You should be My Servant to raise up the tribes of Jacob... I will also give You as a light to the Gentiles, that You should be My salvation to the ends of the earth." The people God set apart from the nations were set apart specifically to be a light to those same nations. Their distinctiveness wasn't the goal. It was the means. A light that stays inside the lamp doesn't illuminate anything. It has to be placed where the darkness is.

Then Jesus spent three years gathering twelve ordinary people, pulling them out of their fishing boats and tax tables and political movements, forming them, teaching them, taking them through their own version of the wilderness. And at the end of that process, in Matthew 28:18-20, He sent them. "Go therefore and make disciples of all the nations." The gathering preceded the sending. The formation preceded the mission. The sanctification preceded the going. That's the pattern. It's not accidental. It's the way God has always worked with the people He calls out.

This matters for something specific that has gone wrong in a lot of Christian communities. There's a version of the call to holiness that quietly becomes an end in itself. A community that's very focused on what it's separated from, very clear about what it doesn't do and doesn't participate in, very careful about maintaining its distinctiveness, but increasingly turned inward. The energy goes toward protecting the community rather than serving the world outside it. The walls get higher. The engagement with outsiders gets thinner. And the whole thing slowly becomes a monastery rather than a mission.

Separation without mission becomes exactly that. Monasticism. Not in the formal religious sense, but in the functional sense. A community that has circled the wagons so tightly that the people outside the circle never experience anything from them except distance. And that's not what God called His people out for. It's a distortion of holiness, not an expression of it.

The corrective isn't to abandon distinctiveness. It's to remember what the distinctiveness is for. You're not holy so that you can stay clean. You're holy so that you can be useful. Salt that stays in the shaker doesn't preserve anything. Light that stays inside the house doesn't illuminate the street. The whole point of the transformation that happens in the wilderness, the reorientation of trust, the stripping of false securities, the cultivation of genuine dependence on God, is that it produces something in you that the world around you desperately needs and can't produce for itself. A person who has genuinely been through the refining process carries something different. And the call is to carry it outward, not to protect it inward.

Think about what this means practically for someone like a hypothetical 36-year-old named Thomas, a high school teacher who has been on a genuine spiritual journey over the past two years. He's worked through a lot of what this book describes. He's named his idols. He's pulled back from the constant digital noise. His prayer life is more honest than it's ever been. He's less anxious, more rooted, more genuinely present to God. And now there's a temptation he didn't expect. He wants to stay in that quiet place. His coworkers feel loud and draining compared to the peace he's found. His neighborhood feels complicated. The messy, compromised world outside his front door feels like a threat to what he's built inside it. What Thomas needs to hear is that the peace he's found isn't a destination. It's a resource. It was given to him for the sake of the people who don't have it yet. The sanctification was for the sending. And the sending is into exactly the spaces that feel complicated and loud and messy, because that's where the light is needed.

First Peter 2:12 says it directly: "Maintain honorable conduct among the Gentiles, that when they speak against you as evildoers, they may, by your good works which they observe, glorify God in the day of visitation." The audience Peter is writing to isn't being told to withdraw from the Gentiles around them. They're being told to live so visibly and honestly among them that even the people who speak against them can't avoid eventually acknowledging what they're seeing. The honorable conduct is meant to be observed. It's meant to be public. It's meant to be the kind of life that raises questions in the minds of people who didn't expect to be asking them.

Philippians 2:15-16 adds the image that captures this most clearly. Believers are to be "blameless and harmless, children of God without fault in the midst of a crooked and perverse generation, among whom you shine as lights in the world, holding fast the word of life." In the midst of. Not removed from. Not protected from. In the midst of a crooked generation, shining. The darkness is the context that makes the light visible. You don't need a light in a bright room. You need it where it's dark. And the people God has sanctified are meant to be exactly that, lights placed in the middle of the darkness, not stored away from it.

The distinct life is the first sermon most people encounter. Before they hear a single word about the gospel, they see how you handle a crisis at work. They watch how you treat someone who can't do anything for you. They notice that you're not anxious in the same way everyone else is anxious. They observe that you have something that looks like genuine peace, genuine generosity, genuine care for people the surrounding culture has decided aren't worth caring about. That observation is what creates the opening. And the opening is what makes the words, when they finally come, land somewhere rather than just pass through.

Sanctification precedes sending. But it has always been in service of sending. The whole point of being made holy is to carry the holiness somewhere it isn't yet. That's the mission. That's what the calling out was always for.

Here's how to put this into practice this week. Spend fifteen minutes in prayer specifically asking God this question: "What did you make me holy for? Who are you sending me to?" Write down whatever surfaces. Not a general category like "my community" or "lost people." Specific names. Specific faces. The neighbor you've been avoiding because their life is complicated. The coworker whose questions about your faith you've been deflecting. The family member whose choices you've been judging from a distance rather than serving up close. Write those names down. Then, for each name, write one specific thing you could do in the next seven days that would put your sanctification to work in their direction. Not a gospel presentation. One act of genuine care. One conversation where you actually listen. One moment where the holiness God has been building in you gets carried outward rather than kept inward.

The Contrast Community

The early church didn't have a marketing strategy. They had no platform, no political influence, no cultural prestige, no access to the corridors of power. What they had was a way of life so visibly different from everything around them that the people who observed it couldn't stop talking about it.

When a plague swept through the Roman Empire in the second and third centuries, most people who could afford to fled the cities to escape contagion. The early Christians stayed. They cared for the sick, including people who weren't part of their community, including people who had no ability to repay them, including people who might have been actively hostile to their faith. They buried the dead when no one else would touch the bodies. They fed the hungry and housed the displaced. And the surrounding culture, which had its own gods and its own religious systems, looked at this and had no category for it.

Tertullian, writing in the late second century, recorded the observation that pagans made about the early Christians: "See how they love one another." That wasn't a compliment delivered by admirers. It was a bewildered observation from people who had no framework for what they were seeing. The Roman world had patron-client relationships, tribal loyalties, family obligations. But a community that extended genuine care across every social boundary, that treated slaves and free people as equals in Christ, that welcomed women and children as full members of the community, that gave sacrificially to strangers, that was something the ancient world simply hadn't seen before.

That visible distinctiveness was the early church's most powerful evangelistic tool. Not its arguments. Not its apologetics, though those mattered. Its life. The way it actually functioned as a community was the thing that made people stop and ask questions. And those questions were the opening for everything else.

This is what the New Testament means when it talks about the church as a contrast community. Not a community that defines itself primarily by what it's against. A community whose way of life is so genuinely different from the surrounding culture that it functions as a living argument for the reality of what it believes. You can dismiss a theological argument. It's much harder to dismiss a community that actually loves people the way it claims to.

The contrast has to be real, though. That's the part that requires the most honest self-examination. It's very easy to perform distinctiveness, to have the right vocabulary, the right positions, the right external markers of Christian identity, while living in ways that are functionally indistinguishable from the surrounding culture in everything that actually costs something. Real generosity that changes your lifestyle. Real fidelity in relationships at a time when commitment has become optional. Real care for people the surrounding culture has decided aren't worth caring about. Real willingness to tell the truth at personal cost. These things are what the contrast is actually made of. Not bumper stickers. Not cultural positions. A way of life.

Galatians 6:10 gives a very specific instruction that captures the shape of this contrast community: "As we have opportunity, let us do good to all, especially to those who are of the household of faith." Two directions simultaneously. Genuine care within the community, the kind of mutual love and service that makes the community itself a visible testimony. And genuine good done to all, extending outward beyond the community to everyone within reach. Both matter. A community that only cares for insiders is a club. A community that tries to serve outsiders without genuine love inside its own walls is a performance. The contrast community does both, and the combination of the two is what produces the effect Tertullian described.

The two extremes that don't work are worth naming clearly, because both of them are live temptations in the current moment. The fortress mentality says: circle the wagons, protect our own, keep the world out, and define faithfulness primarily by what we refuse to touch. That mentality produces communities that are very clear about their boundaries and increasingly irrelevant to everyone outside them. The assimilation mentality says: blend in, don't make waves, be relevant at all costs, and define faithfulness primarily by how acceptable you are to the surrounding culture. That mentality produces communities that are very popular and have nothing distinctive to offer. Neither of these is the contrast community. Both of them are failures of nerve in opposite directions.

The third way is a community so genuinely anchored in Christ that it can enter any space with confidence, neither hiding nor compromising. A community that can sit at the table with people who don't share its values without becoming those people. A community that can engage the culture's questions without being shaped by the culture's answers. A community that offers the world something it cannot produce on its own, genuine love, sacrificial service, fearless truth, and unshakeable hope, and offers it not from a position of superiority but from a position of genuine care.

That kind of community doesn't happen by accident. It's built through the same practices this book has been describing throughout. People who have genuinely dealt with their own idols can love people who are still in the grip of theirs without contempt. People who have been through the wilderness and discovered God's faithfulness there can offer real hope to people in the middle of their own hard seasons. People who have learned to hold their resources loosely can give in ways that actually cost something. The contrast community is made up of people who have been through the sanctification process and are now living out its fruit in the direction of others.

Here's a specific practice to build this into your life right now. Look at your neighborhood or your workplace and identify one person who is genuinely struggling with something. Not a person you're comfortable with. Not someone whose situation is easy to navigate. Someone whose need is real and whose life is messy. Write their name down. Then identify one specific, concrete act of service you can offer them in the next two weeks. Something that costs you time or money or comfort. Not a program. Not a referral to a resource. Something you personally do for them. Then do it without explaining it as an evangelistic strategy. Just do it because you genuinely care about them. That act, repeated with different people over months and years, is how the contrast community gets built one relationship at a time. It's how "see how they love one another" becomes something people in your actual neighborhood can say about your actual community.

The character and conduct of your community is your primary sermon to the world around it. Long before anyone hears you articulate the gospel, they've been watching how you treat people. They've noticed whether your life matches your claims. They've observed whether the community you belong to actually embodies the values it professes. That observation is what creates credibility. And credibility is what makes words land rather than bounce.

Incarnational Presence

Jesus didn't manage the incarnation from a safe distance. He moved into the neighborhood.

John 1:14 says the Word became flesh and dwelt among us. That word "dwelt" in the Greek is the word for pitching a tent. God didn't visit humanity from a position of comfortable separation. He came and set up camp in the middle of it. He ate with people whose reputations made the religious establishment uncomfortable. He traveled to regions that respectable Jews avoided. He touched people the purity codes said were untouchable. He went to the places where the need was, not the places where the approval was. And He did all of this without becoming what the culture around Him was. He was fully present in the compromised spaces of first-century Palestine without being shaped by them. That's the model. Not managed distance. Not fearful withdrawal. Incarnational presence.

This is what presence-based mission actually looks like. The most powerful missionary act available to a believer isn't a program or an event or a well-crafted presentation. It's being a person so genuinely transformed by the gospel that people in your immediate vicinity start asking questions they wouldn't otherwise think to ask. First Peter 3:15 describes this dynamic exactly: "Always be ready to give a defense to everyone who asks you a reason for the hope that is in you." The assumption built into that verse is that people are asking. And people ask because they've observed something that requires an explanation. The hope has to be visible before the question gets asked. The presence has to be real before the defense becomes relevant.

Presence-based mission requires navigating between two extremes that both fail in their own way. The first is assimilation, where you enter a space and gradually become indistinguishable from it. You adopt its values, its rhythms, its definitions of success, its way of treating people, and over time the thing that made you different disappears. You're present, but you're no longer a contrast. You've become the wallpaper. The second extreme is withdrawal, where you maintain your distinctiveness by keeping your distance. You stay in the Christian bubble, interact primarily with other believers, and engage the surrounding culture mainly through critique. You're distinct, but you're not present. You're talking about the darkness from inside a well-lit room with the curtains drawn.

The incarnational model refuses both. It stays present and stays distinct simultaneously. That's the tension that requires the most ongoing attention, because the pull toward one extreme or the other is constant. In certain environments, the pressure to assimilate is enormous. In others, the temptation to withdraw feels like holiness. Navigating between them requires the kind of settled identity that comes from genuine rootedness in God, the kind that was being built through everything this book has covered up to this point. A person who knows who they are and whose they are can enter hostile or compromised spaces without being threatened by them. They're not defensive because they're not insecure. They're not withdrawn because they're not afraid. They're just present, genuinely and fully, carrying something different into the space and letting that difference speak.

Daniel is the clearest Old Testament model of this. He served in the Babylonian government for decades. He worked within the system, interpreted dreams for pagan kings, held administrative authority in the empire that had destroyed his homeland. He didn't treat any of that as a compromise. He treated it as a calling. But he also knew exactly where his lines were. He wouldn't eat the king's food. He wouldn't stop praying. He wouldn't bow to the image. He was fully present in Babylon without being formed by Babylon. His heart was always oriented toward Jerusalem, toward the God who had called him, and that orientation held even when the external pressure to abandon it was enormous. That's incarnational presence. Fully in. Not of.

The practical application of this in your specific context requires honest assessment of two things. First, where are you currently practicing withdrawal under the name of holiness? The workplace conversation you avoid because it feels spiritually risky. The neighborhood relationship you haven't pursued because the person's lifestyle makes you uncomfortable. The civic space you've opted out of because the environment feels too secular. These aren't acts of faithfulness. They're failures of presence. The incarnational model calls you back into those spaces, not to compromise what you believe, but to carry what you've been given into the places that need it.

Second, where are you currently assimilating under the name of relevance? The workplace compromise you've been rationalizing as being a good witness. The social behavior you've adopted to avoid standing out. The values you've quietly absorbed from the culture around you without noticing it happening. These aren't acts of engagement. They're failures of distinctiveness. The incarnational model calls you back to the identity that makes your presence actually matter.

The humility and courage of the incarnation belong together. Humility means you enter the space without superiority, without contempt, without the posture of someone who has arrived to fix the broken people. You come as a servant. You come with genuine interest in the people around you, genuine care for their actual lives, genuine willingness to be present to their pain and their questions without immediately trying to manage it toward a predetermined outcome. Courage means you don't disappear when the pressure to conform increases. You stay distinct when staying distinct costs something. You speak truth when silence would be easier. You maintain the orientation toward God even when the surrounding environment is pressing in the opposite direction.

Paul describes the overall posture in 2 Corinthians 5:20: "We are ambassadors for Christ, as though God were pleading through us." An ambassador lives in a foreign country. They're fully present in it. They learn the language, understand the culture, build genuine relationships. But their ultimate loyalty is always to the king who sent them, and their primary purpose is always to represent that king's interests in the place they've been stationed. They don't become citizens of the country they're stationed in. They don't abandon the country that sent them. They hold both simultaneously, and the holding of both is exactly what makes them useful to both.

That's the identity this chapter is calling you into. Not a visitor who passes through. Not a citizen who assimilates. An ambassador. Fully present. Distinctly different. Carrying something that the country you're stationed in doesn't have and can't produce, and offering it with the humility and courage of someone who knows exactly who sent them and why.

Here's the specific practice for this section. Identify one space in your life, your workplace, your neighborhood, a regular social environment, where you've been practicing either withdrawal or assimilation. Be honest about which one it is. Then make one specific change this week that moves you toward incarnational presence instead. If it's withdrawal, take one step back into genuine engagement with a specific person in that space. If it's assimilation, identify one specific way you've been blending in that costs you your distinctiveness, and stop doing it. Write down what you're going to do and when. Then, once you've done it, pay attention to what happens. Specifically, pay attention to whether anyone asks you a question about why you're different. That question is the opening. And it only comes when the presence is real and the distinctiveness is visible.

What This Looks Like Now: Recap and Your Next Move

This chapter has traced a single arc from beginning to end. God calls people out in order to send them back in. The sanctification that happens through separation, through the wilderness, through the stripping of false securities and the reorientation of trust, isn't the destination. It's the preparation. The people who have genuinely been through that process carry something the world around them needs and can't manufacture. And the call is to carry it outward, into the specific spaces and relationships and communities where God has placed them.

Separation without mission becomes isolation. Mission without separation becomes accommodation. The two have to be held to-gether. The holy defiance this book has been describing from the beginning isn't primarily about what you refuse. It's about what you carry, and where you carry it, and how you carry it. A life so genuinely shaped by the gospel that the people around it can't quite explain it. A community so visibly different in its love and its generosity and its honesty that the surrounding culture looks at it the way those pagans looked at the early church and finds itself asking questions it didn't expect to be asking.

That's the witness. Not a program. A life. Not a platform. A presence. Not a performance of distinctiveness. A genuine transformation that has been carried outward into the specific, ordinary, sometimes messy spaces where you actually live.

The following steps are specific. They're designed to ground everything in this chapter in concrete action starting this week.

First: Identify one neighbor to serve sacrificially in the next thirty days. Not a vague intention to be a better neighbor. One specific person, identified by name, with one specific act of service in mind. It should cost you something real, either time, money, or comfort. Before you do it, pray this specifically: "God, I'm doing this because you sanctified me for sending, and this person is part of where you're sending me." After you've done it, don't explain it as a Christian outreach. Just do it. And then stay available to whatever conversation it opens.

Second: Pray daily for an opportunity to explain your distinct life. Not a prayer for boldness in general. A specific prayer: "God, let someone ask me today why I live the way I live. And when they ask, give me words that are honest and clear and full of the hope that's actually in me." Pray that prayer every morning for the next thirty days. Write down any moment during those thirty days when someone asks you a question about your faith, your values, your choices, or your peace. Those moments are the answer to the prayer. They're the openings that incarnational presence creates. When they come, don't deflect and don't perform. Just answer honestly. Tell them about the hope. Tell them about the God who called you out and sent you back in. Tell them about what the wilderness produced in you that Egypt never could have. That honest answer, given in the middle of a real relationship with a real person who asked a real question, is the most powerful form of witness available to you.

Third: Examine your current community for the contrast it's actually providing. Look at the community you belong to, your church, your small group, your circle of believing friends, and ask honestly: would an outsider observing this community for a month see something they couldn't explain within the categories the surrounding culture provides? Would they see generosity that doesn't make economic sense? Fidelity that doesn't fit the cultural norm? Care for people who can't repay it? Honesty that costs something? If the answer is no, or if you're not sure, that's not a reason to condemn your community. It's a reason to start being the change you're identifying as missing. You can't control what your whole community does. You can control what you do within it. Start there. Be the person whose presence in the community makes the contrast more visible. Be the generosity. Be the honesty. Be the care for the person everyone else has overlooked. One person living this way consistently changes the temperature of the community around them over time.

The whole arc of this book has been pointing here. Not to a more protected version of the Christian life. To a more sent one. The stranger in a culture of compromise isn't strange because they've withdrawn from the culture. They're strange because they're fully present in it and genuinely different from it at the same time. That combination is what the world can't explain and can't stop noticing. It's what made the early church turn the ancient world upside down without an army or a government or a media strategy. It's what's still available to any believer willing to be sanctified for sending, to live as a contrast community, and to show up with incarnational presence in the specific, ordinary spaces where God has placed them.

The mission was always the point. The separation was always in service of it. And the life you've been building through everything this book has asked of you was never meant to be kept to yourself.

14

—·—

THE FINAL CALL

The entire biblical story has been building toward a wedding.

Not a metaphor. Not a poetic flourish. A literal, cosmic, history-ending wedding feast where the Lamb of God takes His Bride and the whole arc of redemption reaches its final, glorious destination. Every chapter of this book has been about preparation for that moment. Every idol named, every prop removed, every act of genuine obedience, every step away from Egypt's comfortable bondage has been the Bride adorning herself for the day she sees her Bridegroom face to face.

Revelation 19:7-8 describes it plainly: "The marriage of the Lamb has come, and His wife has made herself ready. And to her it was granted to be arrayed in fine linen, clean and bright, for the fine linen is the righteous acts of the saints." Fine linen. Clean and bright. That's not imputed righteousness alone, though that is the foundation everything else rests on. It's a life of actual, lived-out obedience. It's the daily decision to crawl back onto the altar when you've crawled off. It's the specific acts of faithfulness that no one else saw but God noticed. It's the money given when it cost something, the truth spoken when silence would have been easier, the idol surrendered when everything in you wanted to keep it. That's the fine linen. That's what the Bride wears to the feast.

Every struggle for holiness you've ever had carries eternal weight. That's not a small thing to sit with.

The Bride Making Herself Ready

The bridal imagery in Scripture didn't start in Revelation. It has roots that go all the way back to the wilderness. Jeremiah 2:2 records God saying to Israel, "I remember you, the kindness of your youth, the love of your betrothal, when you went after Me in the wilderness." God looked back at the Exodus generation, with all their complaining and their golden calves and their desperate longing for Egypt's food, and what He remembered was the love of their betrothal. The going after Him in the wilderness. The fact that they left at all. That they followed the cloud and the fire into a place that had no guarantees except His presence.

That's a stunning act of grace. But it's also a revelation of what God has always been doing with His people. He wasn't just liberating a slave nation. He was wooing a bride. The three-day journey into the wilderness wasn't merely a logistical demand. It was a courtship. God was drawing His people away from the noise and the distractions and the rival gods of Egypt so He could have them to Himself. Ezekiel 16:8 captures it with breathtaking intimacy: God says to Israel, "I spread My wing over you and covered your nakedness. Yes, I swore an oath to you and entered into a covenant with you, and you became Mine." A covenant. A betrothal. The wilderness wasn't punishment. It was the honeymoon.

Paul carries this same imagery into the New Testament without missing a beat. In 2 Corinthians 11:2, he tells the church, "I have betrothed you to one husband, that I may present you as a chaste virgin to Christ." The church is the Bride. The betrothal is real. And the period between betrothal and consummation, which is exactly where we live right now, is the period of preparation. The Bride is making herself ready.

Ephesians 5:25-27 shows what Christ is doing on His side of this preparation. He "loved the church and gave Himself for her, that He might sanctify and cleanse her with the washing of water by the word, that He might present her to Himself a glorious church, not having spot or wrinkle or any such thing, but that she should be holy and without blemish." He's washing her. He's cleansing her. He's removing every spot and wrinkle through the Word and the Spirit. The wilderness seasons, the stripping of idols, the painful exposure of what's been hiding in the heart, all of that is Christ doing what Ephesians 5 describes. He's preparing His Bride. He's making her ready for the feast.

The fine linen of Revelation 19 is woven from the fabric of ordinary days. Not dramatic spiritual experiences. Not conference highs or mountaintop moments. The daily, sometimes unglamorous, sometimes costly choice to be faithful in the small things. The morning you chose prayer over your phone. The conversation where you told the truth instead of managing someone's impression of you. The money you gave when it required actual trust. The bitterness you laid down instead of nursing. The idol you named and surrendered instead of rationalizing. Each of those acts is a thread in the linen. Each one contributes to the garment the Bride will wear at the feast.

Isaiah 61:10 holds this together in a single image: "He has clothed me with the garments of salvation, He has covered me with the robe of righteousness, as a bridegroom decks himself with ornaments, and as a bride adorns herself with her jewels." Both sides of the covenant are present in that verse. The garments of salvation, which are entirely God's gift, and the adornment, which is the Bride's response. You don't earn your place at the feast. But you do prepare for it. And the preparation is the whole-life offering of a person who has genuinely left Egypt and is walking toward the wedding.

Consider someone like a hypothetical 44-year-old named Elena, a nurse and mother of two who has been on a genuine journey of faith for the past several years. She's worked through materialism, pulled back from the digital noise, dealt honestly with some deep-rooted idols of security and approval. She doesn't look particularly impressive from the outside. She's not on a platform. She doesn't have a large following. But she's been faithfully, quietly, consistently choosing the harder thing when the easier thing was available. She's been weaving the linen. And what she might not fully see yet is that every one of those ordinary choices has eternal significance. Every thread matters. The Bride is being prepared, one faithful day at a time, and Elena is part of that Bride.

The three-day journey that began with Moses standing before Pharaoh is ultimately a journey from betrothal to consummation. Every act of faithfulness along the way is the Bride adorning herself. Every step away from Egypt is a step toward the feast. Every idol surrendered is a spot removed from the linen. And the God who called you out of Egypt is the same God who is preparing you for the wedding. He started the work. He'll finish it. Your part is to keep walking toward Him, one faithful day at a time, not a hoof left behind.

The parable of the wedding feast in Matthew 22:1-14 adds an urgency to this that's worth sitting with. The invitation goes out. Many are invited. But the man who shows up without the proper garment, without the fine linen of a prepared life, finds himself speechless before the king. He had no answer. He came to the feast without having made himself ready. The invitation was genuine. The feast was real. But he treated the preparation as optional. That's the warning underneath the beauty of Revelation 19. The wedding is coming. The question is whether you'll be clothed.

The Final Invitation

Something shifts in the final pages of Revelation that most people read past too quickly.

The Bride, who has spent the entire biblical story being called, being wooed, being drawn out of Egypt and through the wilderness and toward the wedding, suddenly changes her posture. In Revelation 22:17, she stops being the one who is called and becomes the one who calls. "The Spirit and the Bride say, 'Come!'" That's a profound transition. Having been separated, purified, and prepared, she joins her voice with the Spirit of God Himself to extend the invitation to everyone still living under Pharaoh's shadow.

She's no longer just the recipient of the call. She's become a conduit for it.

This is the ultimate expression of what holy defiance was always for. The stranger in a culture of compromise isn't strange for its own sake. The separation wasn't an end in itself. The whole point of coming out was always so that the one who came out could turn around and call others to follow. A truly separated person, someone who has genuinely left Egypt's value system behind and been formed by God in the wilderness, becomes a living invitation. Their life is the "Come!" Their generosity, their peace, their willingness to tell the truth, their love for people the surrounding culture has dismissed, all of it is the Spirit's voice speaking through a prepared Bride.

Moses stood before Pharaoh and declared, "Let My people go, that they may serve Me." That was the first call. The beginning of the liberation. And Revelation 19:6 records the response when the liberation is finally complete: "Alleluia! For the Lord God Omnipotent reigns!" The entire sweep of Scripture, from the first demand for freedom to the final shout of triumph, is one long liberation for worship. Every plague, every wilderness trial, every judgment on false gods, every stripping of idols, every step away from Babylon's seductive pull, all of it has been driving toward this: a people finally free to worship the living God without compromise, without distraction, without any rival for their hearts.

That's not just the end of the story. It's the meaning of the whole story. And it's the meaning of your story too.

The person who has genuinely worked through what this book has been asking doesn't just benefit personally from the transformation. They become part of God's final call to the world. When someone who used to be driven by anxiety about money gives with genuine freedom, that's the Spirit and the Bride saying "Come!" When someone who used to need constant stimulation to feel spiritually alive sits in silence before God and finds Him genuinely sufficient, that's the Spirit and the Bride saying "Come!" When someone who used to worship only on Sunday starts treating Monday through Saturday as a continuous offering, that's the Spirit and the Bride saying "Come!" The invitation isn't just spoken. It's lived. And a life that has genuinely been through the Exodus process is one of the most powerful invitations the world will ever encounter.

Song of Solomon 2:10-13 gives the Bridegroom's own voice to this call: "Rise up, my love, my fair one, and come away! For lo, the winter is past, the rain is over and gone. The flowers appear on the earth; the time of singing has come." That's the voice of Christ to His Bride in every generation. Rise up and come away. The winter of Egypt is past. The rain of the wilderness is over. The time of singing has come. The feast is being prepared. The Bridegroom is calling. And the Bride who has heard that call and responded to it can't help but turn around and extend it to everyone still standing in the cold.

This is also where the mission and the holiness finally come together in a single picture. The separated life isn't a fortress. It's a lighthouse. The person who has come out of Babylon's system doesn't stand at a distance from the world, pointing at its failures. They stand at the edge of the light, extending a hand toward the darkness, saying with their whole life: there's something better here. There's a feast being prepared. There's a Bridegroom who is worth leaving everything for. Come.

The final invitation of Revelation 22:17 ends with words that are meant for you personally. "And let him who thirsts come. Whoever desires, let him take the water of life freely." That's the invitation at its most stripped down. No conditions except thirst. No requirements except desire. The Bride who has been prepared by the journey is now extending the same invitation she herself received. Come. The water is free. The feast is ready. The Bridegroom is waiting.

But before you can extend that invitation with any credibility, you have to have responded to it yourself. Fully. Not partially. Not with one foot still in Egypt. The call of this entire book has been asking whether you've actually gone. Whether the departure has been real. Whether the idols have been named and surrendered. Whether the worship has been reoriented. Whether the wilderness has done its work in you. Because the Bride who joins the Spirit's invitation in Revelation 22 is the Bride who has been through everything Revelation describes before that verse. She's been tested. She's been purified. She's been made ready. And now she calls.

That's where this book has been pointing from its very first page. Not just to a better-managed Christian life. To a Bride who is genuinely ready. Who has genuinely left Egypt. Who has genuinely been formed in the wilderness. Who has genuinely been adorned in the fine linen of faithful, costly, daily obedience. Who can stand at the edge of the light and say with her whole life: "Come."

Chapter 14 Recap and Action Steps

The biblical arc that began with Moses standing before Pharaoh ends here. "Let my people go, that they may serve me" finds its ultimate answer in the marriage supper of the Lamb, where a people finally free worship their God without compromise, without distraction, without any rival for their hearts. The three-day journey from Egypt to the wilderness to the place of worship finds its deepest fulfillment in the three days of Christ's passion: Friday's death, Saturday's hiddenness, Sunday's explosion of resurrection life.

Romans 6:3-4 is the theological ground underneath everything. "We were buried with Him through baptism into death, that just as Christ was raised from the dead by the glory of the Father, even so we also should walk in newness of life." The Christian life doesn't just admire Christ's death and resurrection from a distance. It participates in them. Separation from the old life is the Friday. The wilderness of transformation is the Saturday. The emergence into new life and mission is the Sunday. That's your story. That's the three-day journey. Not a metaphor to appreciate but a reality to inhabit.

Paul's deepest aspiration in Philippians 3:10-11 captures what this looks like from the inside: "That I may know Him and the power of His resurrection, and the fellowship of His sufferings, being conformed to His death, if, by any means, I may attain to the resurrection from the dead." Notice that Paul experienced resurrection power before he fully entered the fellowship of sufferings. He wasn't white-knuckling his way through difficulty hoping God would eventually show up. He was already living in the power of the resurrection, and that power was what enabled him to embrace the suffering without being destroyed by it. That's the order of grace. You're empowered before you're tested. You're given the resurrection life first, and then you carry it into the hard places.

We live right now in the Saturday between Christ's first and second comings. A day of hiddenness, of waiting, of faith that doesn't yet see the full picture. The final Sunday, the bodily resurrection and the renewal of all things, is still ahead. But it's certain. The destination is fixed. The Bridegroom is coming. The feast is being prepared. And the Bride is being made ready, one faithful day at a time, in the ordinary and sometimes painful details of a life that has genuinely left Egypt and is walking toward the wedding.

The church is meant to be a third-day people. A community that has passed through death and emerged on the other side. Not triumphalism. Testimony. The marks of the cross are still visible, as 2 Corinthians 4:10-11 says, but the life of Jesus is being made visible through ordinary human bodies. The church's witness isn't primarily a message about a past event. It's a demonstration of a present reality. We have been there. We have died with Him. And we are alive. That testimony is what the world around you has no category for. That's the holy defiance that this entire book has been pointing toward.

Fourteen chapters have covered a lot of ground. Egypt and its idols. The wilderness and its gifts. Worship and its true shape. Materialism and its quiet grip. Fanaticism and its counterfeit urgency. Tradition and its need for honest examination. The mission that sanctification was always preparing you for. All of it has been building toward this moment, which is not an intellectual conclusion but a personal decision. The question this final chapter asks is the same question God has been asking since He spoke to Abraham in Ur, since Moses stood before Pharaoh, since the voice cut through the chaos of Revelation 18. What will you do?

The following steps are designed to bring everything to a decisive personal conclusion. They're not a formula. They're a framework for responding to God with your whole self, not just your agreement.

First: Write your personal covenant of response. This isn't a prayer to repeat or a contract to sign. It's a framework for articulating before God, in your own words, three specific things. Set aside thirty uninterrupted minutes, get a pen and paper, and work through each one honestly. The first is: what am I coming out of? Name it specifically. Not "worldliness" in the abstract. The actual thing. The specific idol, the specific compromise, the specific form of Egypt that still has a claim on your daily life. Name it by its exact function in your heart. What has it been providing that you've been afraid to trust God for? Write that down. The second is: what am I coming to? Describe in one or two specific sentences what faithful Christian living looks like for you in the next season, not in general terms but in the specific details of your actual life. What does it look like to worship God with your Monday as well as your Sunday? What does it look like to hold your resources with an open hand? What does it look like to be present in your neighborhood as someone who carries something different? The third is: what specific step of obedience is the Spirit prompting right now? Not a list of everything you know you should do. One thing. The thing that keeps surfacing when you pray. The thing you've been putting off because it costs something real. Write it down. Then write a date beside it, a specific date within the next seven days by which you'll have taken that step. Keep this covenant somewhere you'll see it regularly. Read it once a week for the next month. Let it be the record of a specific moment when you responded to the final call.

Second: Identify one final area of compromise to lay down. Go back through the chapters of this book and ask honestly: where has the ground shifted but not completely? Where has there been movement but not full surrender? Every person who has read this far has at least one area where the departure from Egypt has been partial rather than complete. It might be in how you spend money. It might be in how you consume entertainment. It might be in a relationship where you've been managing rather than loving. It might be in a tradition you've been protecting rather than honestly examining. It might be in a political identity that's still more central to how you see yourself than your identity as a citizen of heaven. Whatever it is, you likely already know what it is. The fact that it came to mind as you read that sentence is the Spirit's confirmation. Name it specifically in writing. Then pray this prayer out loud: "God, I've been holding this back. Not a hoof shall be left behind. I'm bringing this to the altar. You decide what gets offered." That prayer, prayed honestly rather than ritually, is the Bride making herself ready. It's a thread being added to the fine linen. It matters more than you know.

Third: Answer the three questions of the three-day journey in writing. These three questions, answered honestly, form the substance of your personal testimony and the foundation of your continuing walk. The first question is: where has God brought you out of? Look back at where you started when you picked up this book, or further back if the journey has been longer. What has genuinely changed? What idols have been named and surrendered? What Egypt have you left that you hadn't left before? Write it down specifically. Don't be vague. The second question is: what wilderness are you in right now? What is God currently stripping, testing, exposing, or forming in you? What props are being removed? What is the season of hiddenness or difficulty that you're walking through? Name it honestly. The third question is: what resurrection life is God calling you into? What is on the other side of the current stripping? What does the new thing look like that God is building in the space the idols used to occupy? You may not see it fully yet. Write what you can see. These three questions, answered honestly and revisited every few months, will keep the journey alive rather than letting it become a moment you had once and moved on from.

Finally: Extend the invitation to one specific person this week. The Spirit and the Bride say "Come." You are part of the Bride. That means the invitation belongs to you to extend. Think of one person in your life who is still in Egypt, still running on the world's operating system, still looking for in the wrong places what only God can give. You know who it is. The name is already in your mind. Don't extend the invitation through a gospel presentation or a program. Extend it through one specific act of genuine love this week. Something that reflects the transformation that has happened in you. Something that makes them ask the question that creates the opening. And when they ask, be ready to answer honestly. Tell them about the Bridegroom. Tell them about the feast. Tell them that the winter is past and the time of singing has come. Tell them to come.

The fine linen is woven one thread at a time. The Bride is made ready one faithful day at a time. The journey from Egypt to the wedding feast is walked one step at a time. You don't have to see the whole road. You just have to take the next step that the Spirit is prompting. And the God who called you out of Egypt, who led you through the wilderness, who has been washing and cleansing and preparing you all along, will be faithful to complete what He started.

The feast is being prepared. The Bridegroom is coming. The Bride is making herself ready.

Come.

15

—— • ——

THREE DAYS TO GLORY

The whole story has been moving toward this.

From the moment Moses stood before Pharaoh and asked for a three-day journey into the wilderness, every chapter of this book has been tracing the same pattern. A departure. A stripping. An emergence into something new. That pattern isn't just Israel's story. It isn't just a theological framework you admire from a distance. It's the shape of the gospel itself, pressed into history in the most concrete, irreversible way possible. Three days. A death, a burial, and a resurrection. And everything God has ever asked of His people has been an invitation to participate in those three days rather than just observe them.

Romans 6:3-4 says it plainly: "We were buried with Him through baptism into death, that just as Christ was raised from the dead by the glory of the Father, even so we also should walk in newness of life." The Christian life doesn't just draw inspiration from Christ's death and resurrection. It participates in them. That participation is what this final chapter is about. Not the theory of it. The lived reality of it, what it costs, what it produces, and what it means to keep walking in it when Saturday feels like it will never end.

The Pattern of the Passion

The three-day pattern runs through Scripture like a thread that keeps surfacing in unexpected places. Abraham traveled three days to Mount Moriah before he saw the place of sacrifice (Genesis 22:4). Hebrews 11:19 interprets that journey as a figurative resurrection, because Abraham received Isaac back as from the dead. Jonah spent three days in the belly of the great fish, and Jesus pointed to that directly as a picture of His own burial and resurrection (Matthew 12:40). Esther called a three-day fast before she approached the king, dying to her own safety before stepping into the moment her people's lives depended on (Esther 4:16). Each of these stories follows the same shape. A complete separation. A kind of death. And then something genuinely new on the other side.

But these are all shadows. The substance they were pointing toward is the three days of Christ's passion.

Friday was the death. Not a symbolic death. Not a spiritual metaphor. The actual, physical, publicly humiliating death of the Son of God on a Roman cross outside the city walls. Hebrews 13:12 says Jesus suffered outside the gate, and then draws the implication immediately: "Therefore let us go to Him outside the camp, bearing His reproach." The death happened outside the respectable spaces. Outside the temple. Outside the city. Outside the protection of religious legitimacy and cultural approval. That's where Jesus died. And the call to follow Him there is the call to die to the world in exactly the place where the world's approval gets withdrawn.

This is what "dying to the world" actually means in practice. It doesn't mean you stop caring about people in the world. It means you stop needing the world's validation to feel secure. It means your sense of identity, worth, and belonging stops depending on whether the surrounding culture approves of how you live. That death, like the crucifixion, happens outside the gate. It happens in the places where faithfulness costs you something the world was offering. The career advancement you didn't pursue because it required a compromise. The relationship you didn't pursue because it would have required you to pretend you don't believe what you believe. The silence you broke at personal cost because the truth needed to be said. Each of those moments is a Friday. Each one is a small death outside the gate.

Pharaoh's strategy was always to prevent Friday. His four compromises, which Chapter 1 traced in detail, were all designed to keep Israel from making the complete break. Worship here. Don't go too far. Leave the children. Leave the livestock. Every offer was an attempt to prevent the death that genuine separation requires. The enemy uses the same strategy today. Not outright persecution, at least not always. Just the steady pressure to keep one foot inside the gate, to keep the break from being complete, to keep the death from being final. Because Pharaoh knew what the three-day pattern always produces. And he didn't want Israel to find out.

In Jewish thought, three days was the threshold of finality. A person was considered truly dead after three days, when all hope of resuscitation was gone. That's why Jesus waited until Lazarus had been in the tomb four days before going to Bethany. He waited past the point of no return so that what happened next could only be called resurrection. When God asks for a three-day journey, He's asking for a break that can't easily be reversed. Not because He's harsh, but because genuine transformation requires enough distance from the old system that you actually have to depend on something different. One day is a pause. Two days is a delay. Three days is finality. The old thing is done. Something new is coming.

Moses understood this when he told Pharaoh that not a hoof would be left behind. He didn't know exactly what God would require at the place of worship. He just knew that everything had to come, because you can't predetermine what God will ask for until you arrive at the altar. That posture, bringing everything and letting God decide what gets offered, is the posture of someone who has genuinely died to the negotiating table. It's the posture of Friday. And it's the only posture that makes Sunday possible.

The death Jesus died was also the death of every false identity, every false security, every false source of meaning that humanity had been clinging to. He was crucified outside the gate, which means He was crucified outside the systems of religious respectability, political power, and cultural legitimacy that the surrounding world had built. When you follow Him there, when you let your own version of those things die, you're not losing something good. You're being freed from something that was never actually holding you. The cross doesn't strip away what's real. It strips away what was pretending to be real. And that stripping, painful as it is, is the necessary condition for what happens on Sunday.

Here's how to apply this specifically this week. Take thirty minutes and write down the three areas of your life where the break with the world's system has been the most incomplete. Not in general terms. Specific ones. The area where you're still negotiating with Pharaoh. The hoof you've been leaving behind. Then, for each one, write a single sentence that functions as your Friday declaration: "In this area, I'm dying to the need for [specific thing the world was providing] and trusting God to be that instead." These declarations aren't magic words. They're the beginning of a specific, honest act of surrender that the rest of the three-day journey depends on.

Walking in Newness of Life

Sunday doesn't just undo Friday. Sunday produces something that Friday's world couldn't have imagined.

Romans 6 is the theological center of what resurrection life actually means for a believer. Paul doesn't describe the resurrection as simply the reversal of death. He describes it as the beginning of a completely different kind of life. "Reckon yourselves to be dead indeed to sin, but alive to God in Christ Jesus our Lord" (Romans 6:11). Dead to one thing. Alive to another. The newness isn't a cleaned-up version of the old life. It's a genuinely different orientation, a different source, a different power operating in the same body that went through the death.

This is where resurrection power becomes the most practical thing in the world.

Paul's aspiration in Philippians 3:10 is worth reading carefully: "That I may know Him and the power of His resurrection, and the fellowship of His sufferings, being conformed to His death." Notice the order. The power of the resurrection comes before the fellowship of sufferings. Paul isn't describing someone who endures suffering and eventually earns resurrection power as a reward. He's describing someone who has already tasted resurrection life, and it's that life, that power, that enables him to walk into suffering without being destroyed by it. Grace comes before the test. You're empowered before you're pressed. The Sunday life is available to you before the next Friday arrives, and it's that life that makes the next Friday survivable.

What does this resurrection power actually do in daily life? It does something very specific. It breaks the hold of the old patterns.

Romans 6:6-7 says the old self was crucified with Christ so that the body of sin might be done away with, so that you would no longer be enslaved to sin. The resurrection doesn't just offer forgiveness for the old patterns. It offers freedom from them. Not perfection. Freedom. The power that raised Jesus from the dead is the same power that's available to you when the pull toward the old Egypt is strong. When the materialism whispers. When the entertainment numbs. When the anxiety about status and security starts driving your decisions again. You don't have to go back. The resurrection power is the reason you don't have to go back. And claiming that power isn't presumption. It's exactly what Paul says you're supposed to do. Reckon yourself dead to the old thing. Reckon yourself alive to God. That reckoning is an act of faith, and faith is how resurrection power gets accessed.

The golden calf at Sinai, which Chapter 8 traced in detail, was built by people who had been through the Red Sea but hadn't yet fully inhabited their resurrection identity. They'd left Egypt physically but hadn't yet died to Egypt's way of relating to God. So when Moses was gone and the anxiety rose, they reached back for the familiar form. That's what happens when resurrection life isn't being actively claimed. The old patterns don't disappear just because the departure happened. They have to be actively replaced by the new life. The resurrection doesn't make the old thing impossible. It makes it unnecessary. And claiming that it's unnecessary is the daily work of walking in newness of life.

Think about someone like a hypothetical 31-year-old named Miriam, a graphic designer who came to genuine faith three years ago after a period of significant personal loss. She's been through her own version of the three-day journey. She's named the idols. She's spent real time in the wilderness. But she keeps returning to a specific pattern, a compulsive need for approval from people whose opinion she knows doesn't ultimately matter. Every time she posts her work, every time she enters a social situation, every time she has a difficult conversation, the old anxiety about being found inadequate floods back in. She knows theologically that her identity is secure in Christ. She just doesn't know how to make that knowledge reach the place where the fear actually lives. What Romans 6 offers Miriam isn't more information. It's a practice. Reckon yourself dead to the old identity. Reckon yourself alive to God. Not once. Daily. As many times as the old pattern surfaces. The resurrection power is available every time she needs it. But she has to actively reach for it rather than passively hoping the anxiety will eventually stop.

The worship that flows from resurrection life looks completely different from the worship that comes from religious obligation or emotional atmosphere. Chapter 9 traced the difference between whole-life worship and event-based worship. Resurrection life is what makes whole-life worship possible. A person who is genuinely walking in the power of the resurrection doesn't need a particular atmosphere to encounter God. They don't need the right song or the right lighting or the right emotional state. They've been raised with Christ. The life is already in them. The worship is already happening. What Sunday morning does for such a person isn't create the encounter. It celebrates and renews and expresses together what's already true every other day of the week.

The newness of life Paul describes in Romans 6 is also what enables the mission described in Chapter 13. You can't genuinely serve people you secretly envy or fear. You can't love people you're still competing with. You can't be an ambassador of a kingdom you're not actually living in. But a person who has genuinely been raised with Christ, who is actually walking in the power of that resurrection, carries something into every room they enter that the room didn't have before. Not a program. Not a presentation. A life. The resurrection life is the most powerful evangelistic tool in existence, and it's available to every believer who is willing to actively claim what the death and resurrection of Christ have made possible.

Here's the specific practice for this section. Each morning for the next two weeks, before you check your phone or begin the day's demands, spend five minutes doing what Paul says to do. Reckon. Specifically. Take one pattern, one pull, one area where the old Egypt still has a claim on your daily life, and say out loud: "I'm dead to this. Christ is my life. I'm walking in His resurrection today, not in this." Then identify one specific way you'll express the newness of life in that area before the day is done. Not a dramatic act. One specific thing that reflects the Sunday life rather than the Friday death. Do this for fourteen consecutive days and write down what you notice. The reckoning is the practice. The practice is the walk. And the walk, repeated daily, is what it means to actually live in the resurrection rather than just believe in it.

The Saturday Between

We don't live on Friday. We don't live on Sunday yet. We live on Saturday.

That's the honest description of where the church is right now, in the time between Christ's first and second comings. The death has happened. The resurrection has happened. The power is real. But the final Sunday, the bodily resurrection of all believers and the renewal of all things, is still ahead. And Saturday is a strange, uncomfortable, often disorienting place to live. It's the day when the tomb is sealed and the stone is in place and everything that looked like hope on Thursday night is apparently gone. It's the day when faith has to operate without the confirmation of what's coming. It's the day that requires endurance rather than triumph.

The disciples on the original Saturday didn't know Sunday was coming. That's what made it so devastating. They had watched the death. They were living in the aftermath. The hope they'd attached to Jesus of Nazareth was in a sealed tomb, and they had no framework for what came next. They were scattered, frightened, hiding behind locked doors. The Saturday they experienced was not a day of patient waiting. It was a day of apparent ruin.

We have something they didn't have on that Saturday. We know Sunday came. We know the tomb was empty. We know that what looked like the end was actually the turning point. But knowing that doesn't make our Saturday easy. It makes it endurable. And there's a significant difference between those two things.

The wilderness, which Chapter 12 traced in detail, is the primary biblical image for Saturday living. The Israelites in the wilderness weren't in Egypt anymore. They weren't in the Promised Land yet. They were in between, in the liminal space where the old identity had been stripped away and the new one hadn't fully formed. That in-between space is where God did His most intimate and transformative work. Hosea 2:14 describes it as the place where God allures His people, draws them away from the noise, and speaks comfort to them. The wilderness isn't where God is absent. It's where He's most concentrated. But you have to be willing to stay in it long enough to hear what He's saying, rather than running back to Egypt's familiar noise or demanding that the Sunday come faster than God has appointed.

The Babylon system, which Chapter 3 traced from Babel to Revelation, is what makes Saturday so hard. Babylon is specifically designed to fill the Saturday with substitutes for Sunday. It offers the feeling of fullness without the reality of it. The feeling of arrival without the actual destination. The feeling of meaning and significance and belonging, all delivered on terms that keep you dependent on the system rather than on God. The person who has genuinely died to the world on Friday and is walking in resurrection power from Sunday has something that Babylon can't offer and can't replicate. But they're still living in Saturday. Still surrounded by Babylon's noise. Still facing the daily pressure to reach for the substitute rather than wait for the real thing.

Second Thessalonians 2:1-2 captures the specific Saturday temptation Paul was already addressing in the early church. Don't be shaken. Don't be troubled. Don't let anyone convince you that the final Sunday has already come and you missed it, or that it's so imminent that present faithfulness doesn't matter. Both errors are forms of Saturday avoidance. The first says the story is already over, so why bother with present faithfulness? The second says the story is about to end any moment, so why invest in anything long-term? Both of them produce the same result: a community that stops doing the work of Saturday faithfulness and either retreats into nostalgia or collapses into speculation.

The parable of the wise and foolish virgins in Matthew 25:1-13 is the clearest picture of what Saturday faithfulness actually looks like. All ten virgins knew the bridegroom was coming. All ten were waiting. The difference wasn't knowledge of the timeline. It was preparation. The wise ones had oil. They'd done the unglamorous, unspectacular work of being ready. The foolish ones hadn't. And when the bridegroom came at midnight, no amount of last-minute scrambling could substitute for the preparation they'd neglected. The Saturday life is the oil-filling life. It's the daily, faithful, sometimes boring work of staying ready, not by calculating when Sunday will arrive, but by being the kind of person who is ready whenever it does.

Chapter 6 traced the damage that fear-based eschatology does to this Saturday faithfulness. When the primary energy goes toward figuring out the timeline rather than toward present holiness, the oil doesn't get filled. You can be extraordinarily well-informed about prophetic charts while being extraordinarily unprepared for the Bridegroom's arrival. The wise virgins weren't studying the timeline. They were tending their lamps. That's the Saturday work. Tending the lamp. Staying faithful in the ordinary, daily, sometimes unspectacular work of holiness, generosity, love, and mission.

The Laodicean church, which Chapter 10 touched on in the context of materialism, is the clearest New Testament picture of a community that had lost its Saturday faithfulness. They were comfortable. They thought they were fine. And Jesus told them they were wretched, miserable, poor, blind, and naked, and they didn't even know it. The comfort of Saturday had become a substitute for the preparation that Sunday requires. Their material abundance had filled the space that should have been filled with genuine dependence on God. They'd stopped tending the lamp because they'd convinced themselves the lamp was already bright enough.

Titus 2:12-13 is the apostolic model for Saturday living. The grace of God teaches us to "live soberly, righteously, and godly in the present age, looking for the blessed hope." That phrase "present age" is the Saturday. And the instruction isn't to escape it or to endure it with gritted teeth. It's to live in it. Soberly. Righteously. Godly. With eyes on the horizon but feet on the ground. The blessed hope doesn't produce paralysis. It produces purification. First John 3:3 says everyone who has this hope in Christ "purifies himself, just as He is pure." The certainty of Sunday makes the work of Saturday not futile but urgent. Every act of faithfulness in the Saturday has eternal weight. Every thread of fine linen is being woven right now, in the ordinary details of this present age, for the wedding that is coming.

The manna, which Chapters 11 and 12 both touched on, is the daily provision for Saturday living. It doesn't stockpile. It doesn't come in varieties designed to compete with Egypt's flavors. It just arrives, faithfully, every morning, exactly sufficient for the day. The Saturday life is the manna life. You don't get to see the whole road. You get today's provision. And today's provision is enough, if you've genuinely died to the need for more than God is giving. That's the faith that the Saturday between requires. Not the faith that demands to see Sunday before it will trust. The faith that keeps filling the lamp, keeps eating the manna, keeps doing the work of faithful presence in the specific Saturday you're actually in, because the God who promised Sunday has never once been late.

Here's a specific practice for the Saturday between. Take one area of your life where you're currently waiting. Something unresolved. Something that hasn't arrived yet. Something that requires you to trust God's timing rather than your own. Write down what it is. Then write down the specific act of Saturday faithfulness that's available to you right now in that area, not the act that would be available if Sunday had already come, but the act that's available in the waiting. What does faithful presence look like in this area while you're still in the between? Do that specific thing this week. Not as a way of forcing Sunday to come faster. As an act of trust that the God who promised Sunday is fully present in Saturday and worthy of your faithfulness right now.

Chapter 15 Recap and Action Steps

The three-day journey that began as a request to Pharaoh finds its ultimate fulfillment in the three days of Christ's passion. Friday is the death, the complete break with the old life, the dying to every false security and false identity that Egypt provided. Saturday is the burial, the hidden time of waiting and transformation, the wilderness between what was and what will be. Sunday is the resurrection, the emergence into new life and mission, the power that enables you to walk in a way the old life never could have sustained.

Every theme this book has covered converges here. Separation is the Friday. Wilderness is the Saturday. Worship, mission, and resurrection life are the Sunday. And the Christian life is the participation in all three, not as a one-time event but as the ongoing shape of a life that has been united with Christ in His death and resurrection.

We live in the Saturday between. The final Sunday is certain. The destination is fixed. The Bridegroom is coming. But right now, in this present age, the work of Saturday faithfulness is what's required. Tending the lamp. Filling it with oil. Doing the daily, sometimes unglamorous work of being ready. Not by calculating when Sunday will arrive, but by being the kind of person who is genuinely prepared whenever it does.

The following action steps are designed to move you from the end of this book into the actual living of what it has described. These aren't conclusions. They're starting points.

First: Write a specific "Friday declaration" for the one area of your life where the break with Egypt is still most incomplete. This is the action that everything else depends on. Go back to what surfaced in the Pattern of the Passion section. The hoof you've been leaving behind. The specific area where Pharaoh's compromise still has a grip. Write it down in one specific sentence: "In [this area], I have been getting [this specific thing] from the world's system rather than from God. Today I'm dying to that. Not a hoof shall be left behind." Write the date beside it. Keep it somewhere you'll see it. Read it every morning for the next thirty days. The declaration isn't the completion of the journey. It's the beginning of the Friday that makes Sunday possible.

Second: Establish one daily practice of claiming resurrection power before the day begins. Based on what the Walking in Newness of Life section described, choose one specific old pattern that keeps surfacing, one pull toward Egypt that you face regularly, and build a thirty-second morning practice around it. Before your feet hit the floor, before the phone gets checked, say this specifically: "I'm dead to [the specific old pattern]. Christ is my life. I'm walking in resurrection power today." Then identify one way you'll express that newness before the day ends. Not a dramatic act. One specific thing. Do this for thirty consecutive days. At the end of thirty days, write one honest paragraph about what changed. Not what you think should have changed. What actually did.

Third: Identify your current Saturday and name what faithful presence looks like in it. Every person reading this is in a specific Saturday right now. Something unresolved. Something waiting. Something that requires trust rather than certainty. Name it specifically. Then answer this question in writing: "What does it look like to fill the lamp in this specific Saturday?" Not what it would look like if Sunday had already come. What faithful presence looks like right now, in the waiting, in the between. Write down one specific act of Saturday faithfulness you'll do this week. Something that reflects trust in the God who promised Sunday rather than anxiety about when it will arrive. Do it. Then write down what it cost you and what it produced.

Finally: Pray specifically for resurrection power to fill the area of your life where the old patterns are strongest. This is the most direct application of Philippians 3:10. Paul wanted to know the power of the resurrection. Not as a theological category. As a lived experience. Spend fifteen minutes in prayer, specifically and by name asking God for the power of the resurrection to operate in the area where the old Egypt still has the most pull. Don't pray generally. Pray specifically. "God, I need the power that raised Jesus from the dead to work in [this specific area]. I can't break this pattern in my own strength. I'm asking for Sunday power to operate in my Friday reality." Then sit in silence for five minutes after that prayer and pay attention to what surfaces. Write it down. That prayer, prayed consistently over weeks and months, is what it means to actually walk in the newness of life rather than just agree that it's available.

The three days are your story. Not a metaphor to admire. A reality to inhabit. You've been united with Christ in His death. You're walking in His resurrection. You're living in the Saturday between, with the certainty of Sunday as your horizon. That's not a small thing to carry. It's the most powerful thing a human being can carry into the ordinary details of an ordinary week.

The culture of compromise will keep pressing. Pharaoh will keep offering his four compromises. Babylon will keep offering its substitutes. The world will keep insisting that you don't need to go very far, that you can worship here, that not a hoof needs to leave Egypt. And the answer, now as it was when Moses stood before Pharaoh, is the same. Not a hoof shall be left behind. Three days. All the way. Into the wilderness. Toward the place of worship. Toward the God who is worth every step of the distance between here and there.

That's the holy defiance. That's the stranger's life. That's the three-day journey. And it doesn't end with the last page of this book. It continues tomorrow morning, when you wake up in Saturday and choose, again, to fill the lamp.

16

CONCLUSION

The Resurrected Life: A Summary of Our Journey

You started this book somewhere specific. Maybe it was a vague sense that something was off between what you believed on Sunday and how you lived on Monday. Maybe it was a deeper frustration, the feeling that your faith had stopped moving, that the gap between your professed convictions and your actual daily life had quietly become a permanent fixture you'd stopped expecting to close. Whatever brought you here, the journey these pages have taken you on wasn't accidental.

It started with a number. Three days.

That specific detail from Moses' request to Pharaoh turned out to be the key that unlocked everything else. God didn't ask for a short walk to the edge of town. He asked for three days into the wilderness, far enough that turning back would be a real decision. And as each chapter unfolded, that same pattern kept surfacing everywhere. Abraham leaving Ur. Jonah in the fish. Esther's fast. Jesus in the tomb. The pattern was never just historical. It was always personal. Always a description of what genuine transformation actually requires from a person who wants to worship God in a way that's actually free.

What you've worked through in this book is a diagnosis and a path forward. The diagnosis was specific: most sincere believers aren't walking away from God. They're trying to worship Him without ever fully leaving Egypt. They're holding the name of Christ in one hand and Egypt's value system in the other, and they're wondering why the faith feels hollow. The idols aren't carved from wood. They're made of anxiety about money, hunger for status, dependence on entertainment, attachment to political power, and the quiet comfort of traditions that have never been honestly examined. They don't announce themselves as gods. They announce themselves as wisdom, responsibility, and the reasonable approach to life.

Chapter by chapter, those idols got named.

Mammon was exposed as a genuine rival for the trust that belongs to God alone. The dissatisfaction loop of consumer culture was traced from its source to its effect on the soul. The golden calf pattern in modern worship was named for what it is: sincere people using God's name while borrowing Egypt's forms. The Constantinian trap was identified as the church's recurring temptation to trade prophetic distance for political proximity, and to mistake cultural favor for kingdom advancement. The traditions carried without examination were held up to the Berean standard and found to be a mixed bag, some genuinely apostolic, some merely human, some quietly doing damage to the faith they were supposed to serve.

Fear-based eschatology was distinguished from the hope-driven posture the New Testament actually models. Fanaticism was tested against the fruit of the Spirit and found wanting. The idol of experience was traced from Israel's craving for Egypt's food all the way to the rewired brain that can no longer sit in silence before God. And the wilderness, which most people experience as a problem to be solved, was reframed as the place where God does His most intimate and transformative work in the people He loves.

Then the journey turned outward. Sanctification was shown to be always in service of sending. The contrast community was described not as a fortress but as a lighthouse. Incarnational presence was held up as the model, fully in, not of, carrying something into every room that the room didn't have before. And the whole arc landed where it was always heading: the marriage supper of the Lamb, a Bride who has made herself ready, a people who have been called out so they could be sent back in as a living invitation to everyone still standing in Egypt's shadow.

That's the journey. And it isn't over.

The Call to Defiant Action

The word "defiant" in the title of this book isn't there by accident. It's there because the life being described in these pages doesn't happen passively. It requires a specific kind of courage that the surrounding culture will consistently discourage, misread, and sometimes actively oppose.

It's not the loud, combative defiance of someone who has decided the world is the enemy and their job is to fight it. That's not what this book has been describing. The holy defiance being called for here is quieter than that, and far more demanding. It's the defiance of a person who has genuinely settled the question of whose they are, and who lives out of that settled identity with a gentleness that doesn't waver and a resolve that doesn't apologize.

Moses was gentle with Pharaoh. He wasn't aggressive. He wasn't contemptuous. He just kept returning with the same clear answer to every compromise offered: not a hoof shall be left behind. That's the posture. Gentle. Clear. Unmovable. Not because Moses was stubborn, but because he understood what was at stake and he'd already decided which side of the line he was standing on.

The culture of compromise will keep pressing. It pressed on Abraham in Ur. It pressed on Daniel in Babylon. It pressed on the early church in the Roman Empire. It pressed on the Anabaptists in sixteenth-century Europe. It's pressing on you right now, through your phone, through your bank account, through the social expectations of the people around you, through the political movements competing for your allegiance, through the entertainment that slowly recalibrates what your soul finds satisfying. The pressure is constant. And the only thing that holds against constant pressure is a settled conviction about who you belong to and what that belonging actually requires.

Your distinct life is the most powerful witness you have. Not your arguments. Not your social media presence. Not the positions you hold or the causes you support. The actual texture of your daily life, the way you handle money, the way you treat people who can't do anything for you, the peace you carry in circumstances that produce anxiety in everyone around you, the generosity that doesn't make economic sense, the honesty that costs you something real. That's the witness. And it's available to every believer who is willing to make the departure complete.

The outcomes of that kind of life are real and specific. A soul at peace, not because circumstances are favorable, but because trust is correctly located. A heart full of genuine hope, not the manufactured optimism of someone performing confidence, but the settled assurance of a person who knows how the story ends. A life that points people toward the King not through programs or platforms but through the inexplicable quality of how it's actually lived. These aren't aspirational promises. They're the documented results of people who have made the three-day journey and discovered on the other side that God is exactly who He said He was.

The gentle, unwavering resolve this book calls for isn't something you manufacture through willpower. It grows from the same source that produced it in every person throughout Scripture who walked this path. It grows from genuine encounter with God in the wilderness, from the experience of having your props removed and discovering that He holds what the props were holding, and holds it better. It grows from the daily practice of returning to the altar, reckoning yourself dead to the old patterns, and claiming the resurrection power that's available to every person united with Christ. It grows from community, from belonging to a body of people who are practicing the same reorientation together and holding each other accountable to the life they've committed to.

You don't have to be impressive to live this way. You just have to be honest and willing. Honest about where Egypt still has a claim on you, and willing to let the three-day pattern do its work.

Your Step-by-Step Path Forward

Understanding is not the same as doing. Every chapter in this book has tried to close that gap with specific, actionable steps. This conclusion does the same thing. What follows isn't a vague encouragement to keep seeking God. It's a specific, ordered path for maintaining the holy defiance this book has been describing, one practice at a time.

The first practice is protecting a daily wilderness time of silence, and it needs to be more specific than "spend time with God." Pick a time. The same time every day. Before your phone gets checked, before the day's demands begin, before anything else gets to set the tone. Fifteen minutes minimum. The location matters too. Sit in the same chair, the same corner, the same spot. Your brain will begin to associate that place with the practice of meeting God, which lowers the friction of showing up. During that time, no music, no app, no devotional guide running the show. Open your Bible to a single short passage, read it once slowly, then put it down and sit with it in silence. When your mind wanders, which it will, gently return to the passage. You're not trying to generate insights. You're creating the conditions for the still, small voice to be heard. After two weeks of doing this consistently, write one honest sentence about what changed. Not what you think should have changed. What actually did.

The second practice is a monthly audit of your consumption and allegiances. Not a general resolve to be more intentional. A specific, scheduled review. On the first day of each month, spend thirty minutes going through three categories. Your spending from the previous month, looking for the patterns that reveal where your trust is actually located. Your digital consumption, identifying which sources have been producing anxiety, outrage, or the feeling of insider spiritual knowledge rather than love, peace, and hunger for God. And your allegiances, asking honestly whether any political identity, cultural movement, or institutional loyalty has quietly moved closer to the center of your identity than your citizenship in heaven. For each category, write down one specific change you're making in the coming month. Not a list of resolutions. One change per category, specific enough to describe in a single sentence, concrete enough to know whether you did it.

The third practice is deliberate investment in your local church community as a contrast community. This one requires the most honest self-examination, because it's the easiest to perform without actually doing. Showing up on Sunday isn't the same as investing in the community. Investment looks like knowing people well enough to serve their specific needs. It looks like contributing your actual gifts to the body's actual work, not just attending its events. It looks like being the person whose presence makes the community more generous, more honest, more willing to serve people outside its walls. Identify one specific way you'll invest in your local community this month that costs you something real, time, money, or comfort. Write down what it is and when you'll do it. Then do it. And when the month ends, identify the next one.

The fourth practice is the daily reckoning that Romans 6 describes. Before the day begins, before the phone gets checked and the demands start arriving, take sixty seconds to name one area where the old patterns are pulling and say out loud: "I'm dead to this. Christ is my life. I'm walking in resurrection power today." Then identify one way you'll express that newness before the day ends. Not a dramatic act. One specific thing that reflects the Sunday life rather than the Friday death. This practice sounds almost too simple to make a difference. Do it for thirty consecutive days and then make that assessment. The reckoning is the practice. The practice is the walk. And the walk, repeated daily, is what it means to actually inhabit the resurrection rather than just believe in it.

The fifth practice is the one that ties everything together. Once a week, on whatever day works for your rhythm, spend ten minutes asking God two questions and writing down the answers. The first question is: "What did you make me holy for this week? Who are you sending me to?" The second question is: "What is the one step of obedience I've been avoiding?" The first question keeps the mission alive and prevents separation from collapsing into isolation. The second question keeps the departure honest and prevents the journey from stalling in comfortable familiarity. Write down whatever surfaces. Then act on it before the next week begins. Not eventually. Before the next week begins.

These five practices aren't a program. They're a rhythm. And rhythm is what sustains a life over the long haul when motivation fluctuates and circumstances change and the culture keeps pressing and Pharaoh keeps offering his four compromises. The person who has built these practices into the structure of their week isn't depending on feeling inspired to be faithful. They've built faithfulness into the architecture of their ordinary days.

The wilderness will come again. The props will be removed again. The idols you thought you'd fully surrendered will surface in new forms in new seasons. That's not a sign that the journey has failed. That's a sign that you're still on it. The living sacrifice keeps crawling off the altar. The work of worship is the daily return. And the God who called you out of Egypt hasn't changed His mind about the destination.

The three-day journey ends at the place of worship. Not the worship of an event, but the worship of a life. A life that has genuinely died to Egypt's value system, been formed in the wilderness, and emerged into the resurrection power of a person who knows what they're living for and whose they are. That life is the most defiant thing a human being can offer to a culture of compromise. Not because it's loud or impressive or culturally dominant. Because it's genuinely different. And genuinely different, lived out in the ordinary details of an ordinary week, is what the world has always been unable to explain and unable to ignore.

The Bridegroom is coming. The fine linen is being woven, one faithful day at a time. Not a hoof shall be left behind.

About the Author

Chris Carter has served in pastoral ministry for more than three decades, walking with individuals and families through the joys, sorrows, and stubborn complexities of life together in Christ. Born in Hot Springs, Arkansas, in 1973 and raised as the son of an evangelical minister, he grew up in a home where love for God and lived-out faith were part of ordinary life. During his formative years in northeast Mississippi, the Lord steadily confirmed a call to ministry and to teaching Scripture in ways that touch real Christ-followers where they actually live—not just on Sunday mornings, but in the spaces where faith and culture collide.

Chris's early adult years deepened that call in unexpected ways. While studying at Henderson State University in Arkadelphia, Arkansas, he lived with his maternal grandparents, walking closely with them through the beauty and difficulty of aging and caring for his grandfather as he faced Alzheimer's disease. Those years gave him a firsthand understanding of suffering, dignity, and the kind of dependence on God that no textbook can teach—the same wilderness dependence he writes about in these pages. He later studied Pastoral Ministry at New Orleans Baptist Theological Seminary and Theology/Pulpit Communication at Trinity College and Theological Seminary, grounding a pastor's heart in careful biblical and theological training.

Since 1999, Chris has served as a senior pastor in Mississippi churches, in both fully supported and bivocational roles, and he currently shepherds a congregation in Tupelo, Mississippi. Alongside his pastoral work, he serves as Logistics Manager of Safety and Compliance in the logistics division of a Christian, family-owned building-products manufacturer. This dual calling has given him an unusual vantage point: he knows what it means to preach about leaving Egypt on Sunday and then walk into a Monday workplace where the pressures of materialism, cultural accommodation, and competing allegiances are not theoretical but daily realities. The convictions in this book were not formed in a study alone. They were tested in staff meetings, loading docks, and the thousand ordinary moments where Christ's lordship is either real or decorative.

At the center of Chris's ministry is a conviction that runs through every chapter of this book: God has always called His people out of the world's systems in order to worship Him purely, and that call is as urgent today as it was when Moses stood before Pharaoh. One of his greatest burdens is for believers who love God sincerely yet have unknowingly settled into a comfortable syncretism—blending biblical faith with materialism, entertainment culture, political entanglement, and inherited traditions that have never been examined against Scripture. His writing and teaching flow out of years of preaching, counseling, and countless conversations where the gap between Sunday and Monday was the unspoken crisis in the room.

Chris is also the author of Grace in Everyday Relationships: A Practical Guide for Navigating Everyday Relationships with Grace, and the founder of the Grace in Everyday Relationships blog and podcast. Where that work addresses how the grace of Christ reshapes the way believers speak, forgive, and persevere with one another, A

Three Days' Journey addresses the deeper question of allegiance that makes those relationships either spiritually alive or quietly hollow.

Chris has been married to his wife, Denise, since 1994, and their home has been its own wilderness and proving ground. Together they have raised two children who are now married, welcomed foster daughters into their family, and recently become grandparents. The ups and downs of family life—parenting, fostering, marriage, extended family, and work—have been the context where the truths in this book have been tested, refined, and embodied over time.

Whether preaching on Sunday, leading a team meeting, or sitting at his own dinner table, Chris seeks to live and lead so that Christ's kingdom is seen clearly in ordinary, faithful, Spirit-empowered obedience. His hope for this book is that it will serve as one more voice in the ancient chorus that has echoed from Abraham's tent to Moses at the burning bush to Revelation's final invitation: Come out. Leave Egypt behind. The wilderness is not a punishment. It is the place where God meets His people, strips away what does not belong, and raises them to a life that is genuinely, visibly, and unmistakably new.

www.ingramcontent.com/pod-product-compliance
Lightning Source LLC
Chambersburg PA
CBHW071502140726
47997CB00005B/1826